# DAD'S
# DIARY

# DAD'S DIARY

## 30 DAYS TO BEING A BETTER DAD

## RON ROSE

HOWARD
PUBLISHING CO.
3117 North 7th Street
West Monroe, LA 71291

Our purpose at Howard Publishing is:

- *Inspiring* holiness in the lives of believers
- *Instilling* hope in the hearts of struggling people everywhere
- *Instructing* believers toward a deeper faith in Jesus Christ

### Because he's coming again

Dad's Diary
© 1994 by Howard Publishing Co., Inc.
All rights reserved

Published by Howard Publishing Co., Inc.
3117 North 7th Street, West Monroe, LA 71291-2227

First Printing, April 1994
Second Printing, July 1994
Printed in the United States of America

Cover Design by LinDee Loveland

ISBN#1-878990-29-2

———————————————— ■ ————————————————

*To my father,*
who taught me how to accept responsibility for my own life.

*To my mentors,*
who continue to see more in me, than I do.

*To my girls,*
who keep me humble and connected.

*To my wife,*
who helps me think it's my idea.

*To my God,*
who is so gracious to forgive.

# CONTENTS

# CONTENTS

# PREFACE

Very few men keep diaries, but everyone should. A diary reminds us of how connected we are to other people, especially those we love. The central force driving men today is independence, not dependence, so we politely decline to write, reflect, and connect emotionally. This unnatural expectation, this social pattern is killing us on the inside. It's one reason why twenty-five percent of men in this country are depressed. Like a terminal cancer, this lack of emotional connection is eating away at our souls.

Enough is enough. The wake-up call has come.

Like you, men from every walk of life, from every nook and cranny in America, are openly searching for answers to questions they have never asked before. We fathers have taken the wake-up call, but we're not sure what to do with it. The questions about fatherhood are "what" questions, and they're not simple ones: What to confess? What plans to make? What attitude to change? What wrong to right?

What stories to tell? What confusion to clear up? What motives to check? What victory to savor? What quote to remember? What advice to seek? What action to take? What skill to teach? What limit to set? What encouragement to give? What priorities to change?

*Dad's Diary* is a short course that answers questions. In the next thirty days you will discover what you need to do now, in order to "turn the hearts of fathers to their children and the hearts of children to their fathers" (Mal. 4:6). Nothing can take the place of diary keeping, or journal writing. *Dad's Diary* will give you a concentrated awareness of your impact on the hearts of your kids. In these pages you will learn how to leave a lasting, heart-connected legacy to your children and your children's children.

Here's the process. We begin each day with a passage of Scripture which is followed by a carefully selected insight on fatherhood. The insight is followed by a letter of blessing—the kind of letter a heart-connected father might write to his son, who now has children of his own. And each day ends with a suggested prayer. The rest is up to you. You may want to react, respond, reflect, whatever. You may want to put the book down and "just do it!"

It's time to become the father God wants you to be. Congratulations!

May your tribe increase.

Ron Rose

*Be careful to follow every command I am giving you today, so that you may live and increase and may enter and possess the land that the Lord promised on oath to your forefathers. Remember how the Lord your God led you all the way in the desert these forty years, to humble you and to test you in order to know what was in your heart, whether or not you would keep his commands. He humbled you, causing you to hunger and then feeding you with manna, which neither you nor your fathers had known, to teach you that man does not live on bread alone but on every word that comes from the mouth of the Lord. Your clothes did not wear out and your feet did not swell during these forty years. Know then in your heart that as a man disciplines his son, so the Lord your God disciplines you.*

Deuteronomy 8:1-5

# Training for the Future

Just what is a father supposed to do, anyway? One newspaper columnist described our collective confusion about fatherhood by comparing fathers to the light in the refrigerator: "Every house has one, but no one knows what either of them does once the door is shut." Although a few men seem to do fatherhood "stuff" instinctively; for most, the role of fatherhood is ill-defined. No one sets out to be an absent or apathetic father, but when we don't know what to do, most of us will do nothing, or just enough to get by.

Our only training for *fathering* seems to be self-directed "on-the-job—learn-as-you-go." Just as we learn what to do at one stage, we have to move on to the next. It's pretty tough being confident and consistent when you're making everything up as you go along. At times, we seem to be falling more and more behind, while desperately trying to stay one step ahead. Confusion is a common experience.

Consider this diary your own personal training program. In these pages you will gain confidence and hope—you will learn how to father.

In generations past, home was a haven, a safe place where young and old could recuperate and grow into the people God meant for them to become—it was the training ground for life. Now, too many of us are trying to do home by remote control. No wonder we find ourselves frustrated and exhausted. We can only do fathering "in person"; no one can do it for us.

As I see it, a father does four things. Working with the help of his wife: (1) he provides, (2) he teaches, (3) he leads, and (4) he solves problems.

1. As a *provider,* Dad is responsible for both physical and emotional needs. In short, he provides both house and home.

2. As a *teacher,* Dad introduces his children to the wonder of life. He has the opportunity to teach children how to bait a hook, whistle a tune, snap their fingers, skip a rock, fly a kite, fold a paper airplane, and blow a bubble. If he's wise he will show them how to play Monopoly in less than five hours, how to mow the lawn, how to build a camp fire, how to build a sand castle, how to make a snowman, and how to open a bank account. He will teach them about right and wrong, about God, and about virtue.

3. As a *leader,* Dad sets the standards, the rules of the house. He enforces those rules, and he lives by those rules. Rules are a "must"; they help children feel secure and safe. Sometimes living by those rules requires fathers to sacrifice their own desires for the good of the family, but that's what dads do.

4. As a *problem solver,* Dad helps children overcome their problems and face their enemies. In doing so, he inspires confidence and courage and becomes an everyday family hero. Problem-solver dads always turn into heroes.

When the door is shut, which of these four tasks of fathering do you do best? Which is the most difficult?

Dear Son,

Get a copy of Frank Capra's classic film, *It's a Wonderful Life,* and some evening, when there's no one else around, watch it. View it as a training film for fatherhood. It's the story of an ordinary man who becomes an ordinary family hero. You remember the story? It's about George Bailey who lived his whole life in Bedford Falls, a small a town in America. He never realized his dream to travel the world. He gave it up for civic and family obligations. His only reward seemed to be a growing sense of burden and frustration. Then, when he was threatened with scandal and the possibility of jail because of his uncle's mistake, despair took over. George was saved from hopelessness by Clarence, his guardian angel, who allowed George to see what the world would have been like if he had never been born. Without George, his mother was embittered and suspicious, his uncle went insane, his wife never married, the druggist was a ruined man, and a childhood female friend was a prostitute.

George's heroism consisted not of great adventures, but of doing everyday things with family and friends, regardless of the problems.

I have learned a lot about fatherhood from that movie. I believe you will too.

Love, Dad

# DEAR FATHER,

My request today is that you make me into the father you want me to be. Help me to be your provider, teacher, leader, and problem solver for my kids. Give me strength and skill for the journey.

As you shape and direct my life, help me to shape and direct my children's lives.

In Jesus' name, Amen.

1. What commitments do I need to make?

2. What action do I need to take?

3. What lesson can I pass on to my children?

*No, in all these things we are more than conquerors through him who loved us. For I am convinced that neither death nor life, neither angels nor demons, neither the present nor the future, nor any powers, neither height nor depth, nor anything else in all creation, will be able to separate us from the love of God that is in Christ Jesus our Lord.*

Romans 8:37-39

# Giving Undeserved Love

In 1973, Penn State's John Cappelletti was the Heisman Trophy winner. On the night of the awards banquet, four thousand people crowded into the New York Hilton. John's speech was carefully prepared and held tightly in his hand. John was nervous, but thrilled and honored to be receiving the Heisman.

In his speech, John expressed his gratitude to the Penn State team, his coaches, and Coach Paterno. He told how Coach Paterno had come to his house on a recruiting visit and spent the afternoon with his little brother, Joey. That sensitivity to Joey had played a major part in John's decision to go to Penn State. You see, Joey was battling leukemia. As John started talking about his brother, an unusual hush fell over the crowd. John couldn't hold back the tears. He wadded up his prepared speech and let his heart do the talking.

"If I could dedicate this trophy to Joey, if I could give him one day of happiness, it would all be worthwhile.

They say I have shown courage on this football field, but for me, it is only on the field and only in the fall. Joey lives with pain all the time. His courage is around the clock, and I want him to have this trophy. It is more his than it is mine, because he has been such an inspiration to me."

At the conclusion of those words, every person in the audience stood together with applause and tears. Even reporters can be moved to tears.

Joey was sitting near the front with his dad. He didn't understand what was happening and asked his dad why John didn't want the trophy. Joey's father said, "He wants to give it to you, son."

"But that's not fair," Joey replied. "It's his, he earned it. It's not mine, it's his!"

"I know," Dad said, "but he wants you to have it. He wants to give it to you."

For many of us, the hardest thing in the world is to accept something we don't deserve. We are conditioned to earn everything, to work hard, to pay our dues. But God changed the rules of the game. He gives us his unconditional love at the very times when we desire it the least. And like Joey, we have trouble accepting his gift. Perhaps, that's why I love the words of the country song, "Let me tell you a secret about a father's love, fathers don't love their children every now and then, it's a love without end, amen." I am convinced that the most difficult thing for a father to do is to love unconditionally when he himself has never experienced unconditional love. I need to be reminded daily that God loves me most when I deserve it least. He is my source of unconditional love.

My unconditional love is a gift that only I can give.

Dear Son,

I want you to know, beyond a doubt, that I love you. And I will continue to love you whether you end up a president or a prisoner. There were times when, as much as I wanted to give you other things, I had nothing to give but my love.

Christmas has always been hard for me. As you grew older there was so much I wanted to give you; but the older you got the more expensive the gifts got, and I just didn't have the money. So, as best as I could, I gave you my love.

I know there have been times when you didn't feel loved, when you thought of me as anything but a giver. I hope those memories will fade with time. And I hope you grow to realize that you are loved most when you feel you deserve it the least. That's what I've learned from God.

I pray that you will grow to love giving even more than I do and that you will demonstrate your love for your children, especially when they deserve it the least.

Love, Dad

# DEAR GOD,

Thank you for loving me, even when I didn't deserve it. Thank you for loving me all the time and not just every now and then. It's taken me a long time to realize how much you love me, Lord. I hope you will help me love my kids the same way.

Give me chances to show my kids that I love them unconditionally and the words to tell them so.

In Jesus' name, Amen.

1. What commitments do I need to make?

2. What action do I need to take?

3. What lesson can I pass on to my children?

*You are witnesses, and so is God, of how holy, righteous and blameless we were among you who believed. For you know that we dealt with each of you as a father deals with his own children, encouraging, comforting and urging you to live lives worthy of God, who calls you into his kingdom and glory.*

1 Thessalonians 2:10-12

## Encouraging the Heart

I can't think about encouragement without chuckling over a story told on Arnold Palmer. He was playing in a golf tournament in Omaha, Nebraska. It was the early 1960s, and Arnie's game seemed to be on vacation. His stroke and his attitude had soured. His confidence was unraveling.

By the fifteenth tee box of the final round, Arnie was behind by only three strokes, but to his mind it might as well have been thirty strokes. Then an astounding thing happened. As Arnie addressed the ball at the fifteenth tee, he heard mumbling in the crowd. Some man hidden in the crowd was repeating a phrase over and over, "Arnie can do it, Arnie can do it, Arnie can do it."

Those little words spoken by some anonymous voice gave Arnie an instant shot of encouragement. His confidence returned. He pulled his driver back and slapped that ball straight down the middle of the fairway. It was his best drive in months.

As he studied the conditions in preparation for his fairway shot, he again heard, "Arnie can do it, Arnie can do it." His shot landed three feet from the pin.

Before each shot for the rest of the tournament, Arnie could hear the muffled words, "Arnie can do it, Arnie can do it." Those words changed his game. He birdied the fifteenth, sixteenth, seventeenth, and eighteenth holes, and won the tournament. After he received the trophy, the winner's check, and the accolades of the tournament officials, Arnie heard that muffled voice again. This time the words were different, "Arnie did it, Arnie did it!"

It only took a few moments for Arnie to find the source of those encouraging words. He walked up behind the man, spun him around, and offered a "thank you" hand shake. When the startled stranger tapped Arnie's leg with a white cane, Arnie realized the man was blind. Arnie blushed red with embarrassment. He apologized, but the eager gentleman jumped in and introduced himself. "I'm proud to meet you, Arnie. My name is Charlie Boswell."

After a few moments of uncomfortable conversation, Arnie turned to leave. As a passing comment, Arnie offered, "If I can ever do anything for you, let me know."

"Well, there is one thing," Charlie shot back. "I'd like to play you in a game of golf."

Arnold Palmer looked at Charlie's white cane and said "Uh, how about something else."

Charlie retorted, "How about $1,000 a hole!"

"When do you want to play?" Arnie responded, without hesitation.

"Any night," Charlie answered.

I remember Mel, a preacher from my hometown, putting his hand on my shoulder and saying, "You can do it; you have the gift." He believed in me more than I believed in myself. He could see what I couldn't see, and his words eventually changed my life. He was and still is my "Charlie Boswell." Who is your encourager? Who have you encouraged?

Dear Son,

Your grandfather was my encourager. I remember the day he woke me up before daylight and took me on a walk. We talked of life and work and God and family. I mostly listened, he did most of the talking. We stopped at the donut shop and shared donuts, coffee (it was my first taste of coffee), and more secrets. On the way home, he told me how proud he was of me and what a good young man I was becoming. I'll never forget his words, "You'll have the chance to do things I've never dreamed of, and I know you'll do them well."

Remember when we went fly fishing that first time? We sort of learned "ten and two" together. On that trip, we talked about your dreams. I've thought about those moments a lot, and I want you to know that I believe in you and that I'm convinced you can do it.

When your children come to you with a hope or a dream or something they are struggling with, keep the encourager legacy alive. Sometimes encouragement doesn't require words—it can be passed on in the form of a handshake, a hand on a shoulder, or a hug. But nothing takes the place of the words. Look for opportunities to encourage. We never get enough of it.

Love, Dad

# DEAR LORD,

Thank you for sending encouragers into my life. I still need them in my life, Lord. Give me opportunities to be an encourager to others. Help me to know the right things to say and do that will encourage my friends and family.

Lord, open my eyes to know when my children need encouragement. And help me to teach them how to encourage others.

In Jesus' name, Amen.

1. What commitments do I need to make?

2. What action do I need to take?

3. What lesson can I pass on to my children?

_____

_____

_____

_____

_____

_____

_____

_____

_____

*My son, do not forget my teaching, but keep my commands in your heart,*

*for they will prolong your life many years and bring you prosperity.*

*Let love and faithfulness never leave you; bind them around your neck, write them on the tablet of your heart.*

*Then you will win favor and a good name in the sight of God and man.*

*Trust in the Lord with all your heart and lean not on your own understanding;*

*in all your ways acknowledge him, and he will make your paths straight.*

Proverbs 3:1-6

# Overcoming Deficiencies

Researchers at Boston University have made an interesting discovery. For thirteen years they evaluated a program that trained fathers in what I call "fatherhood stuff." They found that dads seem, naturally and unwittingly, to say or do things that leave their kids thinking, "I should have talked to Mom." The researchers identified the skills men need to develop in order to overcome their fathering deficiencies. Groups of men were trained in these skills, and "presto chango": their kids wanted to talk to them.

This program trained the dads in five specific skills.

1. *Listening to context.* Kids find it hard to tell their dads about fears, worries, or problems, because they aren't sure Dad will understand or even accept how they feel. Dads tend to give advice like, "Don't let it bother you" or "Don't worry about it," shutting down conversation. Men find it easy to forget that our child's initial comments are only the beginning. It takes focused attention to get the context for the comments. So, we need to be more observant, to stop, look, and listen before we speak.

2. *Understanding hidden messages.* Sometimes kids don't know how to express their feelings. Often their strong emotions are acted out in "crazy" behavior. These "crazy" times can be so frustrating that Dad doesn't think about looking or listening for hidden

feelings, he just deals with the craziness. So, feelings stay hidden and craziness continues. Dads who look for hidden messages will cure a lot of craziness.

3. *Practicing self-awareness.* Many dads become uneasy when their kids start describing feelings. Some dads may have deep feelings, unresolved resentments, and frustrations from their pasts that haven't been dealt with. This "baggage" will keep conversations from getting too personal, and many men will unconsciously change the subject, stop listening, blow up and scare the child, or turn cold or distant, just to keep things from getting too personal. To be the dads God intended us to be, we must unpack and put away our baggage from the past.

4. *Exercising self-expression.* Obviously, it's not enough just to be *aware* of our emotions. We've got to learn to put those feelings into words. Generally men don't have a large "feeling vocabulary." So, dads must first find the appropriate words. The search for words takes practice, and wives are usually ready and willing to help in this regard.

5. *Implementing resolution negotiation.* Dads are always tempted to pull rank on the kids, to assert their power, and to intimidate. After all, it's easier and it may be what their dads did to them. In extreme cases it may be necessary, but the normal give-and-take of family relations calls for firm but friendly, sometimes humorous, negotiation.

There is a common denominator in these five skills: they all require time. It's easier to dismiss or ignore our kids, or just hand down an order. But quick solutions don't lead to close relationships, and close relationship is what being a father is all about.

Dear Son,

I remember the day you were born. I held you in my arms, overwhelmed by the wonder of birth. As I handed you to your mother, an unexpected sense of apprehension invaded me. I wasn't sure I had the skills and abilities to be the father you were going to need. I felt so inadequate. Looking back, I needed that humbling time. I needed my eyes and ears tuned to fatherhood.

After all these years, I still wonder about you. I still have uncertainties about my skills. I guess that's okay. But through all the ups and downs of parenting, I have collected bits and pieces of advice that I think are worthwhile.

1. Treat each child as an individual, and bless each one.
2. Invest a part of yourself in each child.
3. Keep growing as a father while your little ones are growing as children.

Love, Dad

# DEAR GOD,

Thank you for the times your Spirit has turned my weaknesses into the strengths my kids needed. I am beginning to realize that we are in this together. I feel like I'm not alone, like I'm part of a team, and I am forever grateful.

Help my kids to listen to my words as I listen to yours. And Lord, thank you for the wonder of it all.

In Jesus' name, Amen.

1. What commitments do I need to make?

2. What action do I need to take?

3. What lesson can I pass on to my children?

_____

_____

_____

_____

_____

_____

_____

_____

*Blessed is he whose transgressions are forgiven, whose sins are covered.*

*Blessed is the man whose sin the Lord does not count against him and in whose spirit is no deceit.*

*When I kept silent, my bones wasted away through my groaning all day long.*

*For day and night your hand was heavy upon me;*

*my strength was sapped as in the heat of summer.*

*Then I acknowledged my sin to you and did not cover up my iniquity.*

*I said, "I will confess my transgressions to the Lord"—*

*and you forgave the guilt of my sin.*

Psalm 32:1-5

# Unpacking Your Bags

After fifty-eight years of life, Bill was living his last days in an elder hostel. His cancer had reached an untreatable level, and even though the doctors were able to help his pain, he was still having a difficult time. Bill's body was rebelling, robbing him of the blessing of dying peacefully. Something inside him was keeping him alive.

The chaplain took the son aside and explained his father's condition. "The doctors are doing everything they can to ease your dad's pain," said the chaplain. "But, I believe your dad has some unfinished business that is keeping him alive. Are you aware of any problems in the past that could be bothering your dad?"

"Yes, I know what's wrong," replied the son. "I am not my father's only child. A number of years ago when my sister was in high school, she decided to get married. She had fallen in love with a boy of a different race, and when she announced their intention to marry, my dad hit the roof. He told my sister that if she married that guy, she'd never be welcome in his house again. She would be disowned. My sister married the guy, and my dad kept his word. Even though she lives less than a hour away, we never talked of her again."

"If you know how to contact her, get her here as soon as possible," the chaplain replied.

Later that evening the young woman who had been disowned thirteen years earlier nervously waited in the elder hostel lobby. Beside her was young Billy, a four-year-old grandson Bill had never seen. After the chaplain explained Bill's condition, the four of them—the chaplain and Bill's son, daughter, and grandson—entered Bill's room together.

Although Bill was confined to the bed by tubes and wires, he was alert enough to recognize his daughter. She was his unfinished business. When she got to his bedside, he looked up at her with tears in his eyes and said in a gentle, hopeful whisper, "I'm sorry. I love you!"

Her only response was, "I know!"

With tears flowing, they hugged as though they would never hug again. They spent the next few hours talking about the good times, catching up on life, and soaking up the moment. They took pictures, lots of them.

Then with everyone gathered around, Bill turned to his son and said, "Thank you for bringing her back." To his daughter, he said, "Thank you for coming." To his grandson, he said, "You'll be a good daddy someday." With his final breath, Bill whispered, "I love you all!" and died.

Bill missed years of good times because he wouldn't turn loose of the past. His unpacked baggage kept him from experiencing some of the greatest joys of life. Unpacked baggage is powerful stuff. Don't waste your life because of pride or anger or bitterness. If you've got some unpacked baggage, do something about it now.

Dear Son,

Forgive me for the times I wasn't there, and for the times I was frustrated about work or the checkbook or my own stupidity, and for the times I took it out on you. I hope you've forgotten the skipped pages in the storybooks, the broken promises, the times I said "not now," the games of catch I was too busy for, and the terrific plays I never got to see. Please forgive me. I make no excuses for my failures. I was just too interested in my own ambitions to see your needs. I messed up, and I'm sorry.

Sometimes adult schedules get so booked with the urgent that we overlook the important. It would be wonderful if we could go back in time and fix the mistakes, the pain, and the abuse, but we can't. In fact, if we spend our lives focused on regrets—"If only I'd done or said . . ."—we will stay stuck in the past. We need to learn from our mistakes, to say—"Next time I'll . . ." Trust me, "next time" is a far better perspective. Please be patient, God's still working on me.

Love, Dad

# DEAR FATHER,

Please forgive me for my past sins. Forgive me for the times I failed you, the times I failed my wife, the times I failed my kids, and the times I failed myself. Help me deal with my unfinished business now, while there is still time. Grant me the courage to confess, like David.

Thank you, Father, for helping me know you have forgiven the guilt of my sin. Now help me feel the release that forgiveness brings. And, Father, help me keep my eyes on the future and not on the past.

In Jesus' name, Amen.

1. What commitments do I need to make?

2. What action do I need to take?

3. What lesson can I pass on to my children?

*They came to Bethsaida, and some people brought a blind man and begged Jesus to touch him. He took the blind man by the hand and led him outside the village. When he had spit on the man's eyes and put his hands on him, Jesus asked, "Do you see anything?"*

*He looked up and said, "I see people; they look like trees walking around."*

*Once more Jesus put his hands on the man's eyes. Then his eyes were opened, his sight was restored, and he saw everything clearly.*

Mark 8:22-25

# Getting a Second Chance

I couldn't believe the thermometer—105 degrees. I was lying on the table in my doctor's waiting room with a thousand milligrams of Tylenol in my system and the highest fever I had ever had. When the doctor walked in, I announced, "Doc, one of three things is going to happen today—you're going to heal me on the spot, I'm going to die here, or I'm going to the hospital."

For the next twenty-eight days, room 325 at Harris Hospital was my home. The first fourteen days were spent testing, probing, x-raying, and puncturing my body. I became a mystery case. A team of six doctors joined forces, trying to solve the mystery fever. Meanwhile, I got weaker and weaker.

Finally, on the fifteenth day, a new doctor entered my room. He introduced himself and handed me his card. "A Definitive Diagnostician" was written under his name. "Surgeon," he said.

"Mr. Rose," he continued, "there are no more tests to give. We know there is a problem in your liver, but we don't know what's causing the problem. Tomorrow we will operate, and I promise you we will stay in there till we find out what's causing your fever."

"By the way," he added, "there is a 50 percent probability that we are dealing with cancer. You need to be prepared for that." With that he handed me some papers to sign and left the room. I was stunned. He had said the "C" word. For the next few hours, time stood still.

I lay there in bed, staring at the ceiling, thinking about potential death at forty-two. My mind was flooded with questions, the tough questions of life and death. I confessed my past mistakes, the ones I could remember and a few I couldn't, just to be sure. I cried, I even tried to deal with God—promising changes in exchange for life. After hours of wrestling with my own fears, I put my headphones on, turned up the volume on my tape player, and let the words of my favorite praise songs fill my head. Gradually the fear was overpowered by my faith. The words of the songs helped me gain perspective and focus. The words, "Because he lives, I can face tomorrow," took on a very personal meaning. I decided that night that I was going to praise God no matter what my future held. If they found cancer, I was going to die giving glory to God. If I got well, my life was going to give glory to God.

The next day they found an anaerobic bacteria. Such a little bitty critter had caused such a big problem. I began treatment, and after a temporary setback with blood clots, I left room 325 and began my "new" life. God had my attention, and he still does. He turned my hospital stay into a "second touch."

I have since decided that my life is filled with start over times, second chances so to speak. I had entered the hospital feeling pretty indispensable and self-controlled; I left the hospital feeling more passion for life, very dependent on God, and much more God directed.

I hope your second touches, your start over times, don't require a hospital stay.

Dear Son,

When you begin to think that you've got life pretty well under control, when you get comfortable, when you think you've planned for all the "what if" contingencies, get ready for a second touch. Now I consider each crisis, each illness, each time of change as an opportunity to touch the hand of God. Mind you, I don't go out looking for these times, but my way of looking at them has forever changed.

At one time in my life, I would have done anything to have protected you from the heartache of these crisis moments, but now my prayer is that you find the hand of God in them. To protect you from pain and tragedy is to keep you away from God's second touches. And I know from experience how life changing his second touch is.

My goal in life is to make God look good no matter what happens to me. I think the religious word for that is "giving glory" to God. I hope you will decide to live your life with a similar goal.

Love, Dad

# DEAR LORD,

Thank you for second touches I have received, and for the third and fourth and fifth touches. Help me keep my heart open to your molding and shaping of my life. Even if I don't act like it at times, I want you to be in control of my life.

And, Lord, help me to learn how to mold and shape my kids the way you mold and shape me.

In Jesus' name, Amen.

1. What commitments do I need to make?

2. What action do I need to take?

3. What lesson can I pass on to my children?

*For this very reason, make every effort to add to your faith goodness; and to goodness, knowledge; and to knowledge, self-control; and to self-control, perseverance; and to perseverance, godliness; and to godliness, brotherly kindness; and to brotherly kindness, love. For if you possess these qualities in increasing measure, they will keep you from being ineffective and unproductive in your knowledge of our Lord Jesus Christ. But if anyone does not have them, he is nearsighted and blind, and has forgotten that he has been cleansed from his past sins.*

2 Peter 1:5-9

# Preparing for the Test

To become a certified public accountant, you have to pass an exam. To become a doctor, an attorney, a journeyman welder, a contractor, a postman, or an engineer, you have to pass a test. We test for mastery of skills and knowledge of details before we let a pilot fly, but there is no test for us to take before we can become dads.

I'm not sure what a fathering test would look like, but I know a few things that would help you prepare for the test. If you know the following things, you will be well on your way to becoming a successful father. As a father you should know

- when to say you're sorry
- how to lose gracefully
- how to tie a Christmas tree to the roof of your car
- how to put your foot down without stepping on toes
- how to make a wrong turn into a short cut
- how to laugh in the middle of a problem

- how to change a car tire
- the punch lines of a few good jokes
- how to win without rubbing it in
- that women don't always know the whereabouts of your lost keys
- how to cook one good meal on a Coleman stove
- how to set up a tent
- how to fold a map
- the art of carving a turkey
- how to cook a decent meal without the microwave
- which day is double-coupon day at which grocery store
- that it's okay to admit you were wrong . . . at least once
- how to control your tongue in front of your in-laws
- how to retell ten Bible stories to your kids
- that your children need to see you being affectionate with their mother
- that sometimes your wife wants you to listen without trying to solve her problem
- that it's okay for men to change their minds too
- that just about the time you think you know what you're doing, your children leave

The real test for becoming a father can't be put on paper. It's not a multiple-choice test of your knowledge. It's on-the-job training. You can know all the right answers, read all the books, watch all the videos, and belong to all the right groups, but if your lifestyle doesn't change with each child, you've flunked the test. Children affect our schedules, our ambitions, our leisure activities, our relationship with God, and our plans for the future. How has fatherhood affected your life?

Dear Son,

When I was a young father, Harry Chapin wrote a song that deeply affected my perspective on fathering. He talked of the day his son was born, "But, there were planes to catch and bills to pay, and he learned to walk while I was away." When his boy turned ten, the son said, "Thanks for the ball, Dad, come on let's play. Can you teach me to throw?"

"I got a lot to do," Dad said.

"That's okay," the boy replied.

I've never forgotten those words. Have you noticed yet, that when your children need you most, you are the busiest at your job, in your office, or at church?

It's tough to do on-the-job training when you're not on the job. Next time we're together, let's play some catch.

Love, Dad

# DEAR GOD,

Thank you for the little things in life. Thank you for things that break that I know how to fix. Thank you for times when I can put my foot down without getting angry. Thank you for camp outs with the kids. Thank you for times when I can tell my kids I'm sorry.

Sometimes, Lord, I wish we could just get together and play some catch.

In Jesus' name, Amen.

1. What commitments do I need to make?

2. What action do I need to take?

3. What lesson can I pass on to my children?

_____

_____

_____

_____

_____

_____

_____

_____

_____

*Therefore we do not lose heart. Though outwardly we are wasting away, yet inwardly we are being renewed day by day. For our light and momentary troubles are achieving for us an eternal glory that far outweighs them all. So we fix our eyes not on what is seen, but on what is unseen. For what is seen is temporary, but what is unseen is eternal.*

2 Corinthians 4:16-18

# Reaching Your Potential

Did you ever get a report card that said, "Doesn't work up to his potential"? I did, and I grew up sure I had something called potential, but uncertain about how it worked, until I met Robert Reed. Now I know.

It had been a long trip, and Gary was tired of driving. He and Robert had been in the car for twenty hours, and the sun was beginning to announce the arrival of a new day. Gary pulled off the road at one of those rest stops, but he couldn't sleep. He found himself sitting there watching Robert sleep.

Robert was amazing. He was a cerebral palsy victim with a spastic body and a heart consumed by a zest for life. His life was spent in a wheelchair. He couldn't do lots of "normal" things. He couldn't walk, drive a car, or feed himself, but Robert was an inspiration to everyone who knew him. Gary took a pen from his shirt pocket and began writing the words of this song:

*Thank you, Lord, for loving me.*
*Thank you, Lord, for blessing me.*
*Thank you, Lord, for making me whole*
  *and saving my soul.*
*Please reveal your will for me,*
*So I can serve you for eternity.*
*Use my life in every way; take hold of it today.*

Robert not only inspired the writing of this wonderful song, he has lived his life living beyond his potential. Robert graduated from Abilene Christian University, became a missionary in Portugal, taught classes at the junior college level, was responsible for bringing over seventy people to the Lord during his six-year stay in Lisbon, Portugal. He married one of his converts and fathered faithful children. Robert did all this with cerebral palsy and a slurred, slow speech pattern that was difficult to listen to, even if you loved him.

Although he is severely limited, Robert has found the secret of living beyond his potential. He loves to do what no one thinks he can do. He loves to surprise his friends. And believe me, he has surprised everyone who has known him. He lives each day to the fullest.

God has blessed Robert with an attitude of perpetual courage. He has an outlook on potential that many whole people will never understand. And his true-life story is a living definition of potential becoming reality.

I thank God for the chance to share a few years with Robert. I hope you know someone like him.

Dear Son,

You, like Robert, are motivated to try things and do things when no one thinks you can. You are motivated by the challenge, the impossible. I have always loved that part of you. When you would take off on some new adventure or tackle some new project, I felt like I was right there with you, doing the impossible.

I'm glad you have learned to live beyond your potential. You don't spend much time thinking about what you have the potential to do—you just do it. You live in the present, not the future, and your kids will be blessed by your practical spirit.

We've all got potential, and we've all got limitations. If we focus on our limitations, whatever they are, our lives will be filled with self-pity. If we focus on our potential, we may never *do* anything. We don't need to talk much about either one; let's just do it. I guess just doing it makes you an inspiration.

That's what your kids need to see.

Love, Dad

# DEAR LORD,

Help me to get my eyes off my potential; it has become my handicap. Help me to keep my eyes on the things that are eternal and important.

Thank you, Lord, for making us whole and giving us limitations at the same time. Thank you for creating us to need you.

Lord, help my children to learn to look beyond their limitations and beyond their potential. Help me to teach them how to serve you, whatever happens to their bodies or their lives.

In Jesus' name, Amen.

1. What commitments do I need to make?

2. What action do I need to take?

3. What lesson can I pass on to my children?

*Sing to God, sing praise to his name, extol him who rides on the clouds—*

*his name is the Lord—and rejoice before him.*

*A father to the fatherless, a defender of widows, is God in his holy dwelling.*

*God sets the lonely in families, he leads forth the prisoners with singing; but the rebellious live in a sun-scorched land.*

Psalm 68:4-6

# Accepting Help

F amily was never meant to be done in isolation. We really need each other. Even the most self-reliant among us needs other people to love, pilots need aircraft mechanics, third-basemen need first-basemen, doctors need nurses, fathers need mothers. In fact, there are times when we just can't do it by ourselves, and fatherhood is one of those times. Maybe this illustration will help.

Dear Sirs,

I am writing in response to your request for additional information. In block number eight on the accident form, I put "trying to do the job alone" as the major cause of my accident. You said in your letter that you needed more details in the report, and I trust the following will be sufficient.

I am an air conditioning/heating serviceman by trade. On the date of the accident, I was working alone on a new, six-story building. When I completed my work, I found that I had about five hundred pounds of tools on the roof. Rather than carry those tools down six flights of stairs by hand, I decided to lower them from the roof in a barrel by rope and pulleys. Securing the rope at the ground level, I then went up to the roof, swung the barrel out, and loaded the tools into the barrel. Then I went back down to the ground and untied the rope, holding it tightly to ensure a slow descent of the five hundred pounds of tools. You will note in block eleven of the accident report that I weigh 135 pounds. You can imagine my surprise when I was suddenly jerked off the ground. I lost my presence of mind and forgot to let go of the rope. Needless to say, I proceeded at a rather alarming rate up the side of the building. In the vicinity of the third floor, I met the barrel coming down the side of the building. This will explain the fractured skull and broken collar bone. Slowed only slightly, I continued my rapid ascent, not stopping until the knuckles on my right hand were buried two inches deep into the pulley. Fortunately, at this time I regained my presence of mind and was able to hold on to the rope in spite of the pain. At approximately the same time, the barrel hit the ground. The bottom fell out of the barrel, dumping the tools, leaving the pile on the ground. With the barrel now empty, and again I refer to block eleven which lists my weight, I began a rapid descent down the side of the building. Again in the vicinity of the third floor, I met what was left of the barrel coming up. This will explain the two fractured ankles and the lacerations on my legs. When I hit the ground, the barrel had slowed me enough that when I fell on the tools, I only sustained three broken vertebrae in my back. I'm sorry that, as I lay on the ground in pain, I again lost my presence of mind and let go of the rope. The barrel came down and broke my hip. I hope that this is sufficient information for the insurance company. Please send a check to me.

Men seem to be bent on self-reliance. Yet, when asked to list who had helped them become better fathers, men responded, "my father," "my wife," and "other men." We were not created to do this fatherhood thing all by ourselves. Strong fathers get help whenever possible.

Dear Son,

I have discovered that, when it comes to fatherhood, a man gets help from his father, his wife, other men, and his God. Many of the men I got help from when you were younger never knew they were helping me. I wanted to appear as though I didn't need the help I had already gotten.

There were times when I was jealous of your time with Grandpa, your teachers, your coaches, and even your mother. I wanted to do it all myself. I wanted to teach you everything. Then your mother helped me see others as helpers, not replacements. Thank God for her wisdom.

I have learned from your granddad that getting help is not a sign of weakness; it is a mark of strength. We were not meant to do this fathering thing alone. We need help from grandparents, other men, wives, friends, and brothers and sisters. After all, family is more than one isolated generation. We all need each other.

Love, Dad

# DEAR FATHER,

Thank you for giving us families. One of the greatest blessings I have received from my family is the realization that I need help. Help me find and be open to the people who can help us be the family you want us to be. Open my eyes to see the people who can help me most.

Help me teach my children that it's okay to ask for help. And help me to become more dependable when they need me. Help us all to learn to depend on you.

And, Lord, thanks again for my wife.

In Jesus' name, Amen.

1. What commitments do I need to make?

2. What action do I need to take?

3. What lesson can I pass on to my children?

*When I shut up the heavens so that there is no rain, or command locusts to devour the land or send a plague among my people, if my people, who are called by my name, will humble themselves and pray and seek my face and turn from their wicked ways, then will I hear from heaven and will forgive their sin and will heal their land.*

2 Chronicles 7:13, 14

# Trying to Be Superdad

In the mid-to-late 1930s, the most notable building project in the San Francisco Bay area was the Golden Gate Bridge. This world famous, record-setting bridge took years to build. On several occasions, its likelihood of being completed was doubtful, to say the least. One of these crisis occasions has become a favorite parable of mine.

Once the two massive towers were completed on both sides of the Golden Gate Straits, the workers began building what was to become the longest single suspension bridge in the world. Millions of miles of cables were stretched back and forth across the water. After the cables were set, they were encased in steel housings. More cables were dropped to the deck below, and a roadway began to take shape. This process was dangerous enough under normal conditions, but the Golden Gate Straits did not provide normal conditions. At times, the wind would gust without warning to sixty miles per hour, swirling from any direction. Catching workers off guard, these strong winds were causing falls that ended in tragedy. The current of the water was so strong that, even if a workman survived the fall to the water, the current would pull him underwater and not release him until his body had reached the Farlan Islands.

At any sign of wind, the work on the bridge stopped; and who has been to San Francisco when it wasn't windy? Fear was causing the best bridge builders in the world to stop working. The workers would slowly, fearfully crawl out on the cable casings; and by the time they reached their work area, it was time to crawl back for lunch. Most of their time was spent protecting themselves from the invisible wind.

At a gathering of workers, it was suggested that a giant safety net be installed under the work area. After all, high-wire performers and trapeze artists worked with safety nets under them. The suggestion was implemented immediately, and as the workers learned to trust the net, they were able to focus on the work of building the bridge. Workers still fell, but the net caught them. A slip of the hand or shaky footing or lack of concentration or a surprising gust of wind would not end in death.

Can you identify with those bridge builders? They were so fearful of misstepping, making a mistake, or being blown away by the changing winds that they did nothing. They spent their time protecting themselves, risking nothing; they were paralyzed by what "might" happen.

Our Father-God is fully aware of our desire to be "superdads." And, he knows that we will fail, that we will get fearful and paralyzed. He knows that the very things we want to do, we will not be able to do, so he changed the rules of the game. He spared no expense in providing a safety net of forgiveness for us, if we will accept it. When we lose our temper, break our promises, or withdraw in silence, he will rescue us and heal our brokenness, if we let him. Because of Jesus, we can get up and start over. For Christians, our failure as fathers is not the end of our influence; in fact, it is the beginning. By turning to God, we teach our children how to do the same. Now, we can all learn from our failures, instead of being doomed by them. Theologians call this "salvation by grace, not by works." I call it good news. Let's bury the pressure-filled "superdad" myth and spread the good news.

Dear Son,

For a while, when you were younger, I was so afraid of saying the wrong thing or doing the wrong thing, that I didn't say or do anything. I had heard so much about how damaging parents can be to their children that I felt it was better just to stop, so I did. I stopped dead in my tracks.

Actually, doing nothing was messing up. If kids never see their parents mess up—if parents never fail—how will children learn to deal with failure in their own lives? And how could anyone ever live without messing up, anyway?

There is no failure that God cannot handle. Nothing can destroy his net. He is the only "superdad." For the sake of your kids, let God help. Accept his forgiveness and trust his net.

Love, Dad

# DEAR FATHER,

Give me a fresh awareness of your transforming power. I fail so many times to be the dad my kids need and the dad I want to be. It scares me.

And free me from the pressure I put on myself to be perfect. Help me to confess my failures to my children so they can learn how to handle their own sins and failures.

Thank you, Father, for the safety net your son provides. I couldn't go on without it. Help me never to take him for granted.

In Jesus' name, Amen.

1. What commitments do I need to make?

2. What action do I need to take?

3. What lesson can I pass on to my children?

_____

_____

_____

_____

_____

_____

_____

_____

*May the God of hope fill you with all joy and peace as you trust in him, so that you may overflow with hope by the power of the Holy Spirit.*

Romans 15:13

# Yielding to God's Hand

Ed came by my office with an offer I couldn't refuse. "I've got a kite. You want to try hang gliding?"

"Do fish have lips? Yes," I responded.

Within minutes, we were headed to the Monterey sand dunes, a perfect place for first-time flyers, where the lift is great and the sand is soft. When we arrived I could see kites lined up ready to soar and lots of people. These people came in every shape and size imaginable. At first we just sat and watched. Soon I zeroed in on one poor fella. He must have tried to get off the ground half a dozen times. Each time, he ended up face first in the sand. It must have been amateur afternoon. No one got his kite off the ground. People were running fast enough, but Ed said they were trying to force the kite to fly. They were trying to push the kite up, instead of letting the kite do the lifting.

By the time it was my turn, I was more than a little concerned about diving face first into the sand. Ed gave me simple instructions. "Let the kite do the lifting. Just push the bar forward and yield to the kite." I didn't know any different, so I did exactly what he said.

I took off down the sand, and at just the right time, Ed yelled, "Now!" I pushed out on the bar, and to my surprise, the kite lifted me up. Before I knew what had happened, I was one hundred feet in the air. It was incredible! I felt like I had wings on my back. Then it hit me. We had talked about how to get up, but we had never talked about how to get down.

I yelled to Ed, "How do I get down?" My thrill of the moment was short circuited by my concern for getting down. Ed responded, "Just keep flying, you're doing fine." Then Ed yelled instructions about how to turn and land. "Remember," he said, "the sand is soft."

I landed without incident, and everybody applauded. I was just glad to be on solid ground.

I flew that day, not because I made the kite fly, but because I yielded to a stronger and higher power. My jumping skills had nothing to do with my kite getting up. My success was totally dependent on my willingness to yield to the kite; and the kite did its job.

Since then I have discovered other times when my success as a father has had nothing to do with my skill or ability. My success, more times than not, is dependent on my yielding to God. He has never failed.

I needed that kite experience. It helped me learn to surrender. As I look back, God has used lots of my experiences to teach me humility and the principle of surrender. How did you learn when to yield?

Dear Son,

Your children need to see you yield to God. They need to know you do what God wants, even when you don't feel like it. They need to know you trust God's word. Tell them this story:

A sun-parched hiker had gone without food and water for three days in the Mojave Desert. As he struggled to reach the shade of a deserted trading post, he feared that this shack might be his dying place. But, to his surprise, hidden by the shack was a water pump!

On the base of the pump was a handwritten note scratched carefully in the weather-worn metal. It read,

> "Under the rocks at the base of this pump you will find a jar of water. DON'T DRINK IT! You will need ALL OF IT to prime the pump. This pump has never failed to give fresh cool water when primed. When you have used all the water you need, refill the jar and bury it for the next person.—Desert Sam."

The hiker clawed his way under the rocks and sure enough there was the jar, full of water. Should he trust this old note and follow its instructions? Tough, isn't it?

Every time you trust God, you are helping your kids develop a legacy of faith. Find ways to do it often.

Love, Dad

# DEAR LORD,

Everyday I am challenged to trust you more, to yield to your direction. I'm sorry for the times I ignore you and go on my own. I am grateful for your patience with me. I still have a lot to learn.

Help me to be as patient with my kids. I want them to trust you even more than I do, so help me show them how to do it. Help me yield to your will and your Spirit with an attitude of joy.

Help me to be more trustworthy myself.

In Jesus' name, Amen.

1. What commitments do I need to make?

2. What action do I need to take?

3. What lesson can I pass on to my children?

_____

_____

_____

_____

_____

_____

_____

*People were bringing little children to Jesus to have him touch them, but the disciples rebuked them. When Jesus saw this, he was indignant. He said to them, "Let the little children come to me, and do not hinder them, for the kingdom of God belongs to such as these. I tell you the truth, anyone who will not receive the kingdom of God like a little child will never enter it." And he took the children in his arms, put his hands on them and blessed them.*

Mark 10:13-16

# Giving the Blessing

We desperately need to restore the father's blessing. It's a mysterious power that seems to be available only to fathers. The father's blessing is a special, significant conversation. It might be a few sentences long or it might fill an afternoon. The words describe the father's vision of his child's strengths, talents, and gifts. The tone is affirming. The setting is usually private and the feelings unforgettable. In his words, Dad paints a picture of the child's present maturity and a vision of what might be. It is much more than a few positive words; it's a heart connection, linking father and child. With the blessing, we are empowered to spend our lives fulfilling our purpose instead of looking for it. Without it, all we have is a collection of wonderful tools, but no reason to use them.

Jerry's dad took him on a father/son camp out that turned into the blessing. "I found manhood in our camp fire talks. I discovered my hopes and dreams because he took time to listen. I began, on that trip, to take responsibility for my own faults and failures because he expected me to. And I saw a new vision for my life because he saw it first. On that trip, he gave me his spirit."

When a father gives his child this blessing, they are connected for life. In giving the blessing a father gives the best of himself so the child can be the best he or she can be.

Many young fathers are still looking for their own blessing. They never received it from their father, so they search for someone else who sees good in them and their future and is willing to tell them about it. Without the blessing, a man feels incomplete. He is never satisfied, and he has this haunting feeling that he has never done enough to be loved.

Feeling truly blessed by our fathers provides energy for life. God gave Jesus a blessing everytime he spoke from heaven.

First, God *claimed* Jesus. "This is my son," he said. In our language, it translates, "Have you met my kids? Stand up, Son. Wave, Sis. If every kid in the world were gathered into one big group, I'd search till I found you. You belong in this family."

Second, God *loved* Jesus. "This is my son, whom I love." The translation is the same: "I love you." Saying the words must be important. After all, God said them.

Third, God *affirmed* Jesus. "This is my son, whom I love, and in whom I am pleased." Think of it this way, "I like the way his life is going. I like how he's growing and what he's becoming." Point out the positive directions in your child's life. That's far more effective than pointing out the bad.

Fourth, God *listened* to Jesus. "This is my son, whom I love, and in whom I am pleased. Listen to him." Today we would say, "Wait, tell me what you think about it. You always have something good to say. I like to hear your ideas."

Every child is looking for the blessing—to be claimed, loved, affirmed, and listened to. Let the restoration begin.

Dear Son,

I never really told you these things before.

You have helped me become a better man, and you have helped me grow closer to our Father-God.

I appreciate the hidden sacrifices that no one ever sees, the things you do when the door is shut.

I have noticed that you are becoming a more nurturing man. I see a side of you that is gentle and sensitive, and I like it very much.

You are in my prayers every day.

I am proud you are my son. I see the person you are becoming. I see his character. I see his heart, and it is good.

You are the next chapter in the continuing story of our family. Write your chapter with power.

These blessings are for you and your children.

Love, Dad

# DEAR LORD,

Thank you for helping me understand more about giving a blessing. I still need to know I am blessed, just like my kids need it.

Help me to bless my kids regularly. Help me to see the good in them and to see the people they are becoming. Help me to notice their strengths, even before they are aware of them. Help me to catch them doing good things for others and to encourage them to continue to do those things.

And help me to pray for them daily.

In Jesus' name, Amen.

1. What commitments do I need to make?

2. What action do I need to take?

3. What lesson can I pass on to my children?

*But if serving the Lord seems undesirable to you, then choose for yourselves this day whom you will serve, whether the gods your forefathers served beyond the River, or the gods of the Amorites, in whose land you are living. But as for me and my household, we will serve the Lord.*

Joshua 24:15

# Saying the Right Words

In 1953, a funny looking pip-squeak named Eugene Orowitz, a high school sophomore who weighed barely one hundred pounds, made a discovery that changed his life. He was a good student as far as grades went, but in every other way this Collinswood High student was desperately searching for some way to fit in.

It was just a normal day until his gym class went out to the school's running track. That day the class tried the hurdles, the broad jump, and the pole vault. Eugene was last in each one.

Then they tried the javelin. As Eugene picked up the gleaming metal spear, he could hear his classmates chuckling, "Don't stab yourself." But with the spear in his hand, Eugene imagined himself as a Roman warrior about to do battle. He raised the javelin over his head, took six little steps, and let the thing go. His throw went straight and true. In fact, it sailed over fifty yards and crashed into some empty bleachers. Nobody could believe what little Orowitz had done. That throw was twice as far as the best throw that day.

When he ran to retrieve the javelin, he found that the tip had broken on the bleachers. Expecting to have to run laps, he brought the javelin back to the teacher.

"Don't worry about. You keep it," the coach said in disbelief.

Eugene did just that. He took it home and never let it out of his sight. By the time he was a senior, he threw the javelin 211 feet, the best throw by a high school boy in the country.

Next, Eugene headed to the University of Southern California, with his dad's words ringing in his ears, "When you've got the chance, do it!" Eugene was on a track scholarship with every intention of being in the next Olympics. Then one day, after not warming up properly, he tore ligaments in his shoulder and discovered he would never be able to throw the javelin again. He gave up his scholarship and his dream of the Olympics, but never gave up on his dad's words.

Eugene turned to acting, and the same feeling came over him that he experienced when he threw that javelin for the first time. After a few years of acting school and small parts, Eugene changed his name to Michael Landon and began a life-changing career playing Little Joe Cartwright on *Bonanza*.

In a news interview conducted just days before his death, Michael Landon spoke of his father's words again. "Whenever I think about what made that scrawny kid pick up that javelin, I know there was a reason. My father was on that high school field whispering to me, 'When you've got the chance, do it!'"

Leave your kids some words to live by. Are you a quotable father?

Dear Son,

Your words make a lasting impression. Plan to leave some your kids will remember for a lifetime. They don't have to be fancy. I really like, "Life will go better if you tell the truth."

I remember when my father questioned me about a broken vase. I wasn't sure if he knew I did it. I thought about denying it and bluffing my way through, but Dad always made such a big deal about telling the truth. I can still hear him saying, "Life will go better if you tell the truth."

I know he wanted me to tell the truth, but I was risking a whipping. There was nothing to do but own up to the broken vase.

I think he hugged me. It was as though I had passed the test. He didn't even punish me for breaking the vase because he was so pleased I had told the truth.

From that moment on, I resolved to take my chances with the truth, although that resolve has been challenged countless times since.

What words of wisdom do you want your kids to remember? Write the words on a card and read that card every day. Then ask God for the opportunity to quote yourself.

Love, Dad

# DEAR LORD,

Help me find and say the words that will be remembered by my children.

Help me to remember your advice, your promises, and your words. Help me to spend more time reading your "Diary." I need to know more of your words in order to have the right words for my kids. Thank you for giving me children who will listen to my words and who remember what I say. They are a blessing to my life.

In Jesus' name, Amen.

1. What commitments do I need to make?

2. What action do I need to take?

3. What lesson can I pass on to my children?

_____

_____

_____

_____

_____

_____

_____

_____

*O my people, hear my teaching; listen to the words of my mouth.*

*I will open my mouth in parables, I will utter hidden things, things from of old—*

*what we have heard and known, what our fathers have told us.*

*We will not hide them from their children; we will tell the next generation*

*the praiseworthy deeds of the Lord, his power, and the wonders he has done.*

*He decreed statutes for Jacob and established the law in Israel,*

*which he commanded our forefathers to teach their children,*

*so the next generation would know them, even the children yet to be born, and they in turn would tell their children.*

*Then they would put their trust in God and would not forget his deeds but would keep his commands.*

Psalm 78:1-7

# Shaping Character

I asked a group of seminar participants to write down the number one value they wanted to teach their children. The overwhelming response was a *personal sense of right and wrong*. *Personal faith* and *caring for others* rounded out the top three. What would your response be?

Parents want children who have strong character—the courage to stand up for their convictions. However, children with strong character seem to be in short supply. We can make a dramatic change in this condition, if we do the following:

1. *Be committed to your marriage.* One of the surest routes to building strong character in children is to bring back marriage—the commitment of a lifetime relationship.

2. *Commit to others.* Your family needs a stronger unifying principle than "making each other happy." Families need a purpose beyond their own, a calling that requires self-denial–serving others, expressing your faith, or helping the helpless.

3. *Commit to the Lord.* Children with strong character are raised in homes where religious devotion is important. These homes are built on traditions and rituals. The only daily ritual practiced regularly in most

American households is "watching television." That *must* change.

4. *Stand for what is right.* When parents decide what their family stands for, what their mission is, what their purpose is, then discipline problems will diminish. Character will return and flourish. What do you stand for?

5. *Revive the practice of family reading.* And don't stop when the kids are old enough to read for themselves. The conversations will be better than any TV program. And family time will become inspirational instead of therapeutic.

6. *Be a good example.* Look for ways to teach morality by the way you live.

Tom, Pauline, and Jason Nichter were wandering the mall in Buena Park, California. Tom had been out of work for five months, but the family was surviving. While on their daily search for food, they found a wallet that contained a $1,500 plane ticket, a wad of $100 bills, and credit cards. To the surprise of the desk sergeant, the Nichters walked into the local police station and turned it in, money and all.

The tourist who lost the wallet rewarded them with a handshake. But after the radio and TV stations and newspapers carried the story, an anonymous well wisher sent them almost $10,000, and a local real estate agent offered them six months' free rent in an apartment.

"All we did was what was right," Pauline said. "We could have used that money, even just a little of it. But we weren't brought up that way, and we didn't want our son brought up that way. We wanted Jason to learn right and wrong. What else could we do?"

Do you believe Jason Nichter will ever forget the lesson about having the courage to live true to your convictions?

Dear Son,

In my day, when a teacher wanted to speak to my parents about my attitude, it usually meant she liked my attitude, even if the grades weren't up to potential. Now if a child has an attitude, it's usually a negative one. When someone spoke of my character, he or she meant I was honest, trustworthy, and kind. Now, character means the child is a comedian or a classroom "cut-up."

It's past time for a character revival in this country, but it will never happen without you and your fellow fathers. Without the leadership of fathers, no character revival will take place. It will take your time, your influence, your teaching, your stories, and your commitment to action. Get a group of fathers together, and ask God to help you begin a character revival in your families, your church, and your community.

I will be praying every day for you and the children. Please join me.

Love, Dad

# DEAR FATHER,

Help me instill deeply rooted, moral convictions in the hearts of my children. Then grant them the courage to live by those convictions. They are pressured on every side, Lord, and they will be challenged. Help them find the courage of their convictions.

And, Lord, help me too. I need courage to live according to your will.

Help me find a group of men who will join with me to pray for a revival of moral character in this country, and help us get others to do the same.

In Jesus' name, Amen.

1. What commitments do I need to make?

2. What action do I need to take?

3. What lesson can I pass on to my children?

*Honor your father and mother—which is the first commandment with a promise—that it may go well with you and that you may enjoy long life on the earth.*

Ephesians 6:2, 3

# Sharing Your Legacy

## DAY 15

My dad was a church-going alcoholic. He only completed eight years of formal education, but he brought home the paycheck, and he paid the bills. He never hit anyone, but he was seldom present as we were growing up. He was either drunk, asleep, or at work. It seems he was worse on special occasions, like birthdays, Thanksgiving, and Christmas. On those days, he was usually just drunk enough to make a scene.

He never drank in a bar. He didn't go out drinking with the guys. He would hide his bottles in the cabinet in the garage or underneath the front seat of the car. During my grade school years, I was embarrassed and ashamed. In junior high, I turned angry and resentful.

Finally I got to the point where I hated his bottle, I hated his slurred speech, and I hated him. The more I expressed my bitterness, the more he drank. Life seemed so unfair. Why did he have to drink? Why couldn't we be like other families? Why couldn't he just stop? I had lots of questions, but no answers.

For twenty-five years, Dad was an unconfessed alcoholic, and the wall between us grew higher and wider.

Until 1978, I was convinced that Dad had taught me nothing, that I had grown up cheated out of time and wisdom, and I was determined I would not be guilty of doing the same. Then the impossible happened. He checked himself into a treatment center, spent thirty-five days learning to be sober, and never drank again. The next four years were dedicated to cautiously rebuilding our broken relationship.

Then, on October 29, 1980, my dad died. I remember slipping out to my dad's workshed. There in that little junk filled room I felt his presence. For hours, he and I and God talked.

I told him about my fears, my resentment, my failure, and my sense of being disconnected and left behind. All those pain feelings poured out. During our talk, that room became my junk room too. When I walked out, I walked free. God took my stuffed resentment and bitterness and kept it locked within the walls of the workshed.

I still miss my father, but now I realize I am his legacy. I am alive to tell his story; in fact, I am his story, volume two. You, too, are your dad's legacy. It is your task to find the best in three generations, in him, in you, and in your children. Then, once you have found it, tell someone the story.

Dear Son,

Don't let your kids forget their grandparents. Tell them about us and tell them about great-grandparents, too. Tell about our failures and our successes. Be honest. In telling our stories, you honor us and give us extended life. Tell about our adventures, our embarrassing moments, our crises, our victories, our hopes, our dreams, our unusual relatives, and our courage.

Get us all together for a family history-telling weekend and tape record our stories. (Hurry, before long we'll forget some of the best stuff.) Make your next reunion a videotape production. Your kids will love it.

Get the kids to interview us about what it was like when we were youngsters. It will challenge us to remember those days and will be a great time for the kids. In fact, it would be fun to let us interview the kids, too.

Take lots of pictures, and get double prints. We will do the same. Pictures help us tell the more recent stories. After all, life is still going on, and our family story is still being written.

Thanks for keeping the legacy alive.

Love, Dad

# DEAR LORD,

Thank you for my father, for his strengths and his weaknesses. Thank you for making me an extension of his life. Give me opportunities to tell my children about him, about his adventures, his struggles, and his victories. He made it possible for me to know you, and for that I am forever grateful.

Help me to act in such a way that my children will find joy in honoring me. Help them to remember me in positive ways long after I'm gone.

Thank you for a legacy of love.

In Jesus' name, Amen.

1. What commitments do I need to make?

2. What action do I need to take?

3. What lesson can I pass on to my children?

*Now we ask you, brothers, to respect those who work hard among you, who are over you in the Lord and who admonish you. Hold them in the highest regard in love because of their work. Live in peace with each other. And we urge you, brothers, warn those who are idle, encourage the timid, help the weak, be patient with everyone. Make sure that nobody pays back wrong for wrong, but always try to be kind to each other and to everyone else.*

*Be joyful always; pray continually; give thanks in all circumstances, for this is God's will for you in Christ Jesus.*

*Do not put out the Spirit's fire; do not treat prophecies with contempt. Test everything. Hold on to the good. Avoid every kind of evil.*

*May God himself, the God of peace, sanctify you through and through. May your whole spirit, soul and body be kept blameless at the coming of our Lord Jesus Christ. The one who calls you is faithful and he will do it.*

1 Thessalonians 5:12-24

# Learning From Grief

I hope I never have to face the tragedy Gary Lee experienced, but I have learned from him and his grief. I think you will, too. Gary's son, a sixteen-year-old junior, was quiet and shy. His teachers said they enjoyed him as a student because he was sweet and never disrupted the class. They did frequently comment that he would not apply himself to his studies and often daydreamed.

Gary's son had an ongoing struggle with math. Algebra I and Geometry were barely passed after much effort, including lectures, forced completion of homework, and numerous counseling sessions. Then when he failed the first semester of Algebra II because he didn't do the homework, he was told he must maintain a C average, or he would be required to have a tutor.

On February 4, Gary's son received a failing test grade in Algebra. Gary was angry and frustrated because his son didn't even do the homework. "I told him I would arrange for a tutor," Gary said, "and he left the room visibly upset and depressed." Later Gary agreed to his son's suggestion that they work on the homework together, rather than get a tutor. And they agreed to begin homework as soon as they finished supper.

Gary left the room and went to the kitchen. Less than five minutes later, a single gunshot changed everything.

"I will never know," Gary cried, "why my son took his life. He never told me his feelings or if he was disturbed by other events. Nor did he tell his feelings to other family members, teachers, or even his best friends. I've learned the hard way that you can't always protect them, and you can't teach experience. We have to let our children make their own mistakes and learn from them just as we did. If we tell our children how much we love them and how proud we are of them, in spite of their mistakes and imperfections, perhaps it will help carry them through the rough times. Tell your children how important they are to you and how much they are loved. Tell them often."

Gary still feels the pain of knowing that his final words to his son were the words that sparked his death. Had he known his son's feelings, his words would have been so different, and the boy would never have been left alone in his despair.

"For my son," says Gary, "I can only say words which would have meant so much when he was alive, but now seem empty and meaningless: 'I love you, Kevin, and I'm sorry.'"

We need to hear these words. We need to hear the words of fathers who have experienced the grief of life, because we can learn much from them without having to go through those valleys ourselves. They want to share with us; they want their stories to make a life-changing impact on our lives. Gary's has!

Dear Son,

I have lunch twice a month with Cecil, a longtime friend. We share good food, wholesome humor, and each other. He knows my feelings, my opinions, my dreams, my beliefs, my fears, and my failures. He's a buddy. We have talked about problems, jobs, family, and the Lord. When one of us faces a crisis, the other one feels the pressure. This kind of friendship is extremely valuable. You don't find it often.

We listen. We encourage. We hold each other accountable. We share resources. And, over the years our families have come to share the New Year's tradition together. We bring out the best in each other, and I need that.

When tragedy hits, when life seems to cave in around me, Cecil helps me feel the hand of God. He helps me look for the other side of the coin, another perspective. I thank God for that.

You need a friend like that. Sure your wife should be a friend, but there are times when you need the relationship of another man. Take the time to invest yourself in more than casual conversations about sports, or hunting, or work. Find a buddy like Cecil, and your family will be blessed. And you will learn a lot about yourself.

Love, Dad

# DEAR GOD,

I need faithful men who will help me live the way you have called me to live. Please give me brothers who will love me, encourage me, and challenge me. I need men to whom I can be accountable. I pray you will send such a man or group of men into my life soon.

I am grateful for my wife and our growing friendship, but I need brothers who will help me become what you want me to be. Sometimes I need a warning, sometimes an example, and sometimes lots of encouragement. Thanks for making church the place where I can find these brothers.

Lord, as my children grow up, help them to find friends who will encourage them to stay close to you.

In Jesus' name, Amen.

1. What commitments do I need to make?

2. What action do I need to take?

3. What lesson can I pass on to my children?

*Therefore I am now going to allure her; I will lead her into the desert and speak tenderly to her.*

*There I will give her back her vineyards, and will make the Valley of Achor a door of hope.*

Hosea 2:14-15

# Romancing Their Mother

When I first got married, I was convinced that romance was just the first step to having sex. I knew at least one or two others who felt the same way. After several disappointments and some heated discussions, I finally discovered another perspective—my wife's. To her, romance is touching her in nonsexual ways, giving her a back rub, touching her cheek, combing her hair, planning a picnic and taking care of the details, and surprising her when she least expects it.

A romantic will do whatever it takes to clear the cobwebs from his heart and speak thoughtful words like the following (and say them often):

> "Put on your best dress. I'm taking you out for a surprise evening."
>
> "Let's take a walk together. Just the two of us."
>
> "You are always so thoughtful (sensitive, caring)."
>
> "I love your eyes (hair, legs, skin)."
>
> "You're the best wife a man could hope for. You're my best friend."
>
> "When I think about you, I get a warm feeling all over."
>
> "I'm taking your car in for new tires because I don't want you to have any trouble with flat tires while you're out driving."

"I'm going to run an errand. Is there something I can get for you while I'm out?"

"It's just a little something I brought you to say I love you."

A romantic man will always help his wife to remember that he loves her more today than the day they got married. One romantic had just bought "the" car of his dreams. His wife took the car on an errand and got tangled up with another car. With tears in her eyes, she got out and surveyed the damage. She had no idea how she would be able to face her husband.

The driver of the other car asked for the registration and insurance information, so she reached into the glove box and found a note attached to the needed documents. In heavy masculine scrawl the note read,

"In case of accident, remember, Honey, it's you I love, not the car."

*That* is a "romantic" note.

The most important thing a young father can do for his kids is to love their mother. Nothing builds a child's security like knowing his parents are really in love with each other, and nothing influences the child's perceptions about marriage more than Mom and Dad's marriage.

Take your wife on a date once a week, making sure you get out of the house and do something together without the kids. It doesn't have to cost money, but it has to cost your time and presence, your heart, and your involvement. And take care of all of the arrangements yourself.

Write notes, not just anniversary, birthday, Christmas, or Valentines notes, and not a Hallmark card either, but a note from you—short and simple and signed.

Romance is only romance when it's a surprise. Do something surprising. Put some spark, some excitement back into that young marriage.

Dear Son,

Words of advice:

When your wife comes home with a new hairstyle don't say, "What'd you do to your hair?" or "Boy, that looks better."

When she tells you that your habit of leaving your dirty underwear on the floor two feet from the hamper is driving her nuts, don't tell her your mother never complained about it.

When she is in the kitchen dumping pasta into a colander, turning down the heat under boiling vegetables, cutting up lettuce for the salad, reaching for the beeping microwave oven, talking with her mother on the phone, and your eighteen-month-old announces from the next room that she has to go potty, don't say, "Go tell Mommy."

Whatever it takes, do something now to break the silence. Learn to be surprisingly romantic.

Love, Dad

# DEAR LORD,

Help me keep romance alive in my marriage. Help me to find the words that explain my desires and my needs. Help my wife to understand what I say and what I can't say.

Please keep the sexual part of our love exciting and fulfilling, but help me find ways to keep the feeling part of our love just as exciting.

Lord, teach me to talk to my wife about my dreams, my fears, my intentions, and my feelings. And help us turn the stresses and troubles of our family into a "door of hope." Help us find pleasure in each other, just as you intended.

Then, Lord, help us show our children what romance and marriage are supposed to be like.

In Jesus' name, Amen.

1. What commitments do I need to make?

2. What action do I need to take?

3. What lesson can I pass on to my children?

*Praise be to the God and Father of our Lord Jesus Christ, the Father of compassion and the God of all comfort, who comforts us in all our troubles, so that we can comfort those in any trouble with the comfort we ourselves have received from God. For just as the sufferings of Christ flow over into our lives, so also through Christ our comfort overflows. If we are distressed, it is for your comfort and salvation; if we are comforted, it is for your comfort, which produces in you patient endurance of the same sufferings we suffer. And our hope for you is firm, because we know that just as you share in our sufferings, so also you share in our comfort.*

2 Corinthians 1:3-7

# Challenging Your Hope

On June 20, 1985, Jack Carter, his son Dave, and his grandsons, Dustin and Caleb, went to Yellowstone for a much anticipated, wilderness camping trip. While they were boating across the lake, a freak storm came up, and the wind and waves capsized their boat seventy-five yards from shore. They found themselves separated in thirty-five degree water trying to swim toward the shoreline, while the wind and the waves pushed them away from it.

Jack saw Dustin just a few feet away and got him to a floating seat cushion. Together, they hung on. From that point on, Jack never saw Dave or Caleb again.

"I knew the cold water had already brought sleep to Caleb," Jack said later.

For a while the waves seemed smaller, and the two of them slowly moved closer to the shore. Dustin was still alert, so very brave.

He kept saying, "We're going to make it, Grandpa. I know we're going to make it." Then his words started slurring and came less frequently. Jack urged him to keep talking and to keep his eyes open. Dustin tried so bravely for so long, but the freezing water finally brought sleep to him as well. Jack tried to keep Dustin's face out of the water, in hopes he would be able to revive him when they reached the shore.

Jack recalled, "My right arm rested on the cushion and my right hand held Dustin. We were only a few yards from the shore, when the dashing surf ripped the cushion away. I did what I could to reclaim Dustin, but I could not close my fingers on his clothing."

A wave drove Jack against a tree, and he rested there. Jack had been in the water nearly three hours, and it was dark when he finally pulled himself along the tree and felt rocks beneath his feet. In total exhaustion, he crawled inland enough to find shelter between two fallen trees. The luminous dial on his watch indicated it was just past eleven o'clock.

The next morning, Jack stumbled across a patrol cabin, and within an hour he was at Yellowstone hospital. They found the lifeless forms of the boys right away. It was two weeks before they found Dave's body.

"I watched almost indifferently as the doctors and nurses worked to restore my circulation and body temperature," Jack remembered. "They seemed to care a whole lot more than I did. Occasionally one of them would remark about my strength and how it had saved me. I was too weak to tell them how wrong they were. I could only remember how futile my efforts had been. I could still see Dustin's face sinking into the water as my strength failed. My strength helped no one."

Within hours, one of Jack's daughters, her husband, a niece, and a nephew were by his side. Their presence kept Jack from total despair.

The next day, while Jack was at the Cody airport waiting to be transported home, he met Dave's wife, Marsha, and her father as they were arriving to make final arrangements for the bodies. The embrace of that moment helped lift a great portion of Jack's burden.

Looking back on this terrible tragedy, Jack sees no reasonable explanation for his survival. I believe he's still alive to share the story and give us hope. If God can help people through times like that, God can help your family through anything.

Dear Son,

I have learned that God is my greatest source of help when the really tough times hit. When I come to the end of my rope, God is always there. I might not understand the "whys," but a long time ago I promised to trust him, and so I do. I may never understand "why," and I have come to accept that.

I hope that your trust in God will help you find hope when the circumstances seem hopeless. I have found that regardless of how tragic the circumstances, God always lights a candle of hope.

Love, Dad

# DEAR GOD,

You know I don't like the tough times. I don't like the pain and the grief. And there are times when it feels like you are unapproachable. My mind tells me you will always be there, but my heart feels alone.

When the unbearable experiences happen, please help me find your comfort fast. Help me take that comfort and find a way to help someone else feel it. I know you have given it to me, not to keep, but to share.

Then help me learn how to help my children discover your presence in the middle of troubles. They will be blessed to discover early in life that you are the source of real comfort.

In Jesus' name, Amen.

---

1. What commitments do I need to make?

2. What action do I need to take?

3. What lesson can I pass on to my children?

*The end of all things is near. Therefore be clear minded and self-controlled so that you can pray. Above all, love each other deeply, because love covers over a multitude of sins. Offer hospitality to one another without grumbling. Each one should use whatever gift he has received to serve others, faithfully administering God's grace in its various forms. If anyone speaks, he should do it as one speaking the very words of God. If anyone serves, he should do it with the strength God provides, so that in all things God may be praised through Jesus Christ. To him be the glory and the power for ever and ever. Amen.*

1 Peter 4:7-11

# Living With Interruptions

Gene Stallings has coached some of the most famous football teams in America. He is used to making a game plan and doing what it takes to follow the plan. But even the best game plans have to make room for unexpected interruptions. This famous coach, loving husband, and honored father learned about interruptions in a very personal way.

When Gene's son Johnny was born, he did more than interrupt their schedule. He interrupted their dreams, their faith, and their lifestyle. He was born with Down's syndrome. The doctors told the family that Johnny would probably not live a full life, and Gene was encouraged to place Johnny in a home for retarded children. After all, that would be the easiest thing to do.

However, as troubling as Johnny's condition was, the Stallingses refused to institutionalize Johnny. They brought him home, and he has lived at home since.

"We made a decision when we brought him home that he would be part of the family. We go to church, we bring him. We go to the country club, we bring him. We decided we weren't going to hide him," Gene said.

Other than Gene, Johnny is the most famous Stallings. He and his father have been seen across the nation on a United Way commercial. Johnny's interruption has become a gift that now has been shared with more than just the family. Johnny has helped thousands. God has used Johnny and his family as encouragement for other handicapped children across this country.

The human perspective is to see interruptions as problems and difficulties. God sees these interruptions to our game plan as opportunities to show us his power. I remember hearing a wise man say, "I used to ask God to take away all the interruptions, all the distractions. I felt that the only way to get close to God was to have a life free from interruption. Finally, I realized that the interruptions were my life."

Fathers are called by God to lead their families through the interruptions, whatever they are. The task is awesome, but the rewards are unbelievable. Fathers who look for God in the face of life's interruptions will leave a legacy that is unmatchable in this lifetime. It will be a legacy from the heart of God.

Dear Son,

I love strategic planning. Analyzing what the present situation is and projecting what problems will be faced in the future helps me feel prepared. Examining the cultural trends, the outside influences, and the major issues expected in the next five years gets me ready for action. Assessing the critical issues, the operational issues, and the developmental issues makes major decisions easier. Clarifying which issues are success producers and which ones are failure preventers gives me confidence. And communicating the actions in the most effective way at the most effective time gives me a "strategic planner's high."

As much as I think it would help every father to develop a strategic plan for his family, the impact of such a plan is not nearly as powerful as your reaction to the interruptions of life. You will be remembered for your reactions, not your hours of planning.

For a while I tried to plan away all interruptions, and I got very frustrated.

Finally, I decided that the interruptions weren't messing up my life, they *were* my life. I see life as an adventure filled with daily interruptions. Some are big ones, some are ever so slight, but life is learning how to shape those interruptions without having them shape you.

So, plan the trip, but don't let it get in the way of the adventure.

Love, Dad

# DEAR FATHER,

Help me to live by your agenda and not mine.

Help me to be more patient with the interruptions of life, and help me to be more open to your will in those interruptions.

Grant me the courage to see unexpected events and personal suffering as opportunities to grow closer to you. Give me oil for my lamp when the days get dark. And, Lord, send someone to help when I am at the end of my rope.

Help me teach my children to find hope and faith hidden somewhere in the interruptions of our lives.

In Jesus' name, Amen.

1. What commitments do I need to make?

2. What action do I need to take?

3. What lesson can I pass on to my children?

*My dear brothers, take note of this: Everyone should be quick to listen, slow to speak and slow to become angry, for man's anger does not bring about the righteous life that God desires. Therefore, get rid of all moral filth and the evil that is so prevalent and humbly accept the word planted in you, which can save you.*

*Do not merely listen to the word, and so deceive yourselves. Do what it says. Anyone who listens to the word but does not do what it says is like a man who looks at his face in a mirror and, after looking at himself, goes away and immediately forgets what he looks like. But the man who looks intently into the perfect law that gives freedom, and continues to do this, not forgetting what he has heard, but doing it—he will be blessed in what he does.*

James 1:19-25

# Controlling Your Anger

Joe was taking a college course in ornithology, the study of birds. He had signed up for the course because the professor never checked roll. Joe had also heard that the only test was a multiple choice final that could easily be passed by cramming the night before. Thus Joe would be able to add three hours of credit to his transcript with minimal effort.

Joe only attended two lectures all semester, and he didn't even buy the textbook. He was certain he would be able to cram enough bird knowledge into his head the night before to pass any multiple choice test, so he prepared for the final with confidence. The night before the final, Joe nearly memorized the textbook he had borrowed from the library. He walked into class ready for bear.

Joe took a seat in the front row. Upon arrival, the first thing the professor did was place a large box on the lab table. From the box, he pulled out ten little cloth sacks. Each sack held a stuffed bird he had brought from his own bird collection. The only thing sticking out of the sacks were legs. It was a funny sight. There on the lab table were ten little sacks with two legs sticking out of each sack. A string was tied around the mouth of each sack, hiding everything but the legs of the bird.

The professor had numbered the sacks one to ten. Finally, he said, "I got tired of multiple choice tests, so this semester your final is simple. Examine the legs sticking out of these sacks. Identify the name of the bird, give its common name, genus, species, habitat, mating habits, etc. Tell me everything you know about each bird. You have two hours, so work wisely."

Joe was in shock. "This isn't fair," he thought.

He walked past each little sack, trying to find something that would give him a clue, but he drew an absolute zero. They all looked the same. And the more he stared at those legs, the angrier he got, and the more hopeless it all seemed.

He sat there for thirty minutes, seething. Finally, he reached his boiling point. He stood up, marched to the professor's desk, slammed his exam paper down in front of the professor, and marched to the door. The professor was stunned for a moment, then looking at the blank paper, he called out, "Wait a minute, young man! You didn't put your name on this paper. What is your name?"

In a moment of brilliance, Joe turned around, lifted one leg up high in the air and shouted, "You tell me, you tell me!"

Joe defused his anger by blasting someone else. Truth is, he wasn't really mad at his professor; he was mad at himself. His professor was innocent, but got blasted anyway.

At times, we are all like Joe when we're angry. It isn't our kids we're angry at, but they're the ones who get blasted. In fact, some kids know more about what makes their father angry than they know about his life.

How do you handle your anger? Is there a better way?

Dear Son,

I must tell you about the great mask that men wear. While many of us appear to be warm and confident on the outside, we are masking an overwhelming sense of defeat. We may have great trophies that indicate we are worth something, but awards don't reveal how we feel as men. We are angry because we can't find our soul. I used to be like that.

I felt I had to be self-reliant and dependent on no one. When my father died, I felt distant and disconnected. When someone asked, "What's wrong?" I snapped, "Nothing!" It seemed my role in life was all focused on being in control—at work, in sports, and in arguments.

Finally, while walking with my wife one evening on a long stretch of beach, the mask slipped off. I opened up and the real me poured out. The only time I had talked before was in anger. Now I was saying things I'd never told anyone, and she loved me anyway. My silence was finally broken.

My anger still blazes to the surface once in a while, and when it does, I know it's time for a long talk. Now I know what love is. I hope you know what I'm talking about.

Love, Dad

# DEAR GOD,

I don't know what to do with my anger. I wish I could wrap it up in a sealed container and give it to you. Please hear my concerns, and help me get rid of this burden. I have decided to spend more time talking to you about it, so get ready for some intense times in the future.

Help me to be slower to snap at my kids. Help me to listen first.

God, help me to get rid of my competitive spirit. It's so easy for me to turn everything into a game.

God, help me to show my kids how to talk about my anger without hurting feelings or people.

God, I am ready for whatever it takes.

In Jesus' name, Amen.

1. What commitments do I need to make?

2. What action do I need to take?

3. What lesson can I pass on to my children?

*God also said to Abraham, "As for Sarai your wife, you are no longer to call her Sarai; her name will be Sarah. I will bless her and will surely give you a son by her. I will bless her so that she will be the mother of nations; kings of peoples will come from her."*

*Abraham fell facedown; he laughed and said to himself, "Will a son be born to a man a hundred years old? Will Sarah bear a child at the age of ninety?" And Abraham said to God, "If only Ishmael might live under your blessing!"*

*Then God said, "Yes, but your wife Sarah will bear you a son, and you will call him Isaac. I will establish my covenant with him as an everlasting covenant for his descendants after him.*

Genesis 17:15-19

# Laughing a Lot

In *7 Things Kids Never Forget,* I told about a first-grade girl who asked her mother why her father brought home a briefcase filled with work papers every evening. Her thoughtful mother replied, "Daddy has so much work to do at the office that he can't finish it all."

After a moment of silence, the little girl wondered, "Well, why don't they just put him in a slower group?"

I hope you're laughing. One of a father's most important possessions is his sense of humor, his ability to laugh at life and himself.

One father told of watching his son demonstrate exciting skateboarding skills. A burst of youthfulness came over this middle-aged father, and he began to imagine himself zipping around on that skateboard.

"Yo! Dad!" his son called. "Come on—it's fun. Try it, you just get on it and go."

After a moment of courage-gathering, Dad agreed, and, with the help of his son, he stood up on the board.

"Now," his son instructed, "make it move!"

This apprehensive dad kept his right foot on the board, balanced on it, and pushed with the left until he got to the downhill slope of the driveway. The rest is a blur. The board shot out from under him, and he went flying through the air, landing with his full weight on the side of one foot.

"Wow, Dad! That was radical. Do it again."

On the way to the hospital, his son retold every detail of the flying skateboard ride. He told everyone in the emergency room how neat it was.

The doctor on call walked up, took one look at the foot, and responded rather critically, "Riding a skateboard at your age . . ."

"But it was quality time!" the father replied.

Learning to laugh at our own mistakes is one of the greatest lessons in life and one we teach best by our example. If we are willing to risk failing in front of our kids, and can laugh when we aren't successful, we teach them to have the courage to try new things and not to be devastated or defensive when it doesn't work out like they've planned.

Dear Son,

Humor is one of the most valuable assets in life. Share it with everyone.

You can coax a chuckle out of a twelve-month-old just by putting a Frisbee on your head. Any self-respecting baby knows that a Frisbee is not a hat. It's a teether.

When a baby is eighteen months old, you can get a laugh with slapstick antics—Dad tripping, toys falling, and destruction in general are all funny to toddlers.

Toddlers want you to be their audience. Sometimes they will fall down on purpose to get you to laugh.

At five years, children begin to make up their own riddles. They will memorize and repeat riddles before they really understand them. To them, a homegrown joke that was funny the first time becomes absolutely uproarious the forty-first time.

During the elementary years, sitting in the back of the car and shouting, "Your girlfriend's a gorilla!" is worth loads of laughs.

Take the time to tell and retell funny stories about family members. It helps everyone feel connected. Remember, for every slapstick artist, there has to be a straight man.

Love, Dad

# DEAR LORD,

Help me learn to laugh at myself and not at others. Help me keep fun and laughter alive in our home.

Open my eyes, Lord. I want to give my children a sense of humor. I want them to know you are a God who encourages laughter. I want them to know that Abraham and Sarah laughed, and I want them to know that it was okay with you.

Thank you for the gift of humor. Help me to use it wisely. In Jesus' name, Amen.

1. What commitments do I need to make?

2. What action do I need to take?

3. What lesson can I pass on to my children?

*Not that I have already ob-
tained all this, or have already
been made perfect, but I press on
to take hold of that for which
Christ Jesus took hold of me.
Brothers, I do not consider myself yet to have taken hold of it.
But one thing I do: Forgetting
what is behind and straining toward what is ahead, I press on
toward the goal to win the prize
for which God has called me
heavenward in Christ Jesus.*

Philippians 3:12-14

# Winning by Running

For years, Bill Rogers competed in marathons and 10Ks across this country. But the 10K he ran in Omaha, Nebraska, proved memorable for a reason other than victory. It was in Omaha that Bill Rogers met Bill Brodus. Brodus, a middle-aged Omaha resident, made the local 10K a run worth remembering. He had a respiratory problem that limited his ability to run longer than five minutes. Every step taken after five minutes caused a mixture of pain and panic in Brodus' body. But he loved to run, and it was Brodus' dream to run in the same race with Bill Rogers. Rogers was his hero.

When the Omaha 10K was announced and the paper reported that Bill Rogers was going to run in it, Brodus went straight to his doctor. After consulting with the doctor and arranging to have family and friends stationed all along the route, Brodus prepared to make his dream come true.

When the starting pistol fired, Bill Rogers was in the front. Bill Brodus was far in the back, about as far back as you could get. Rogers won the Omaha 10K without much problem. And after he crossed the finish line, it was easy to lose track of who had finished.

Brodus was still running.

The cleanup crew removed the ropes and the temporary stands.

Bill Brodus was still running.

The broom pushers swept up all the Gatorade cups.

Brodus was still running.

There was nobody at the finish line. There was no finish line. Finally Brodus rounded the corner, each step filled with pain and struggle. But he was about to finish the race, the same race that his hero, Bill Rogers, had run. Just before Brodus reached the spot where the finish line would have been, Bill Rogers and Bill Brodus' family stepped out into the lane.

Bill Rogers took a strip of the broken finish line he had crossed earlier and held it out in front of Brodus. Brodus saw the line and lunged across it, falling into Bill Rogers' arms. Rogers took the medallion that he won that day, placed it around Brodus' neck, and whispered, "Today, you're the winner." Bill Brodus wasn't a winner because he came in first. He was a winner because he endured pain and struggle to see his dream come true. He kept running, even when the steps were filled with pain.

The winner's medallion was unexpected. It was a gift. I am convinced that our greatest victories as fathers are not because we finish first or because we're the fastest or the strongest. The greatest victories come because we keep on going, even when it gets painful and discouraging. Remember, on Friday night it looked like Jesus had lost, but on Sunday the picture was totally different. Jesus has already won the race. We just have to run.

Dear Son,

There will be times when you don't feel like staying around. You will feel trapped and tied down. On occasion, you will have the opportunity to break free, to bolt for the door. Your wanderlust will grow strong, and you will dream of being free of responsibility, free of burdens, free of relationships, free of expectations, free of hands expecting money, free of complaints, free of demands. Your heart will deceive you. I know. Believe me, I know.

The mark of a strong man is not that he lives according to his heart or that he lives for happiness and good times. The mark of a strong father is that he lives by his word, keeps his promises, and stays on the track when he doesn't feel like it. That spirit of endurance and commitment is one of our greatest needs today.

I've discovered that if you keep running, God changes your heart.

I love the way he works.

Love, Dad

# DEAR LORD,

Help me keep my eyes on the goal and not get discouraged or distracted. I really need help with endurance and keeping a sharp focus.

Help me to keep running, even when I don't want to. Please grant me the strength to live up to my promises and my commitments.

Forgive me for the times I have failed.

In Jesus' name, Amen.

1. What commitments do I need to make?

2. What action do I need to take?

3. What lesson can I pass on to my children?

*You, however, know all about my teaching, my way of life, my purpose, faith, patience, love, endurance, persecutions, sufferings—what kinds of things happened to me in Antioch, Iconium and Lystra, the persecutions I endured. Yet the Lord rescued me from all of them. In fact, everyone who wants to live a godly life in Christ Jesus will be persecuted, while evil men and impostors will go from bad to worse, deceiving and being deceived. But as for you, continue in what you have learned and have become convinced of, because you know those from whom you learned it, and how from infancy you have known the holy Scriptures, which are able to make you wise for salvation through faith in Christ Jesus. All Scripture is God-breathed and is useful for teaching, rebuking, correcting and training in righteousness, so that the man of God may be thoroughly equipped for every good work.*

2 Timothy 3:10-16

# Nurturing Their Faith

As a father, you are the most significant spiritual teacher your child will ever have. You will help shape and mold your child's personal faith in Jesus. Your task requires more than knowing the right answers to spiritual questions. It requires nurture, prayer, patience, and a few struggles along the way.

Think of faith-shaping as a process much like the transformation that happens inside a cocoon. The little caterpillar begins by being a ground-loving, crawling creature, but he escapes from his cocoon transformed into an untrained, full-time pilot with a permanent pair of wings. He truly is a new creation. For the rest of his life, he will be discovering what has already happened to him.

Within the darkness of that cocoon, a mysterious, God-ordained process was free to work, unaffected by outside pressures or threatening circumstances. At just the right time, driven by nature's design, the caterpillar died to "caterpillarness" and was changed into a butterfly.

Once the transformation is complete, the "struggle" begins. The "new creature" must leave the safety of the cocoon. He must leave his security and fly, for that's what he was meant to do.

As fathers, we can't start or stop this process, but we can help shape it. To a great extent, we are the most significant faith-shapers our children will ever have. You can begin faith-shaping through these eight simple practices:

1. *Accept your kids as they are.* Intensify the practice of accepting your kids where they are, not where you wish they were. Give your children the freedom to fail and grow. Living in this kind of environment gives your children a secure base from which to build their faith.

2. *Discipline yourself.* Maintain the discipline of personal Bible study. Consider the Bible as the Diary of God and study it to learn more about the God who wrote it. One of the best ways to grow closer to Him is to spend time reading His Diary.

3. *Listen to your kids during the unstructured times.* Those informal meandering conversations will give you a chance to share concerns, conflicts, and failures. Listen for understanding, not information. Listening may be the best kept secret of effective fathers.

4. *Encourage them to question and search.* Real faith is never developed without a testing period—a time of challenge, question, and crisis.

5. *Practice grace-filled fathering.* We are called to care and teach, not to cure and judge.

6. *Tell stories about faith-filled people.* Storytelling gives you the opportunity to share powerful moments with your children. Stories can help you turn your limited quantity of time into potential quality time.

7. *Invite your children to join you in prayer.* Ask them what they would like you to pray for and tell them what you want them to pray for. Children love to know that they are being prayed for.

8. *Share your conversion story with your children.* Tell them what you were thinking about when you decided to give your life to God. Describe what happened at your new birth, who was present, and what happened afterward.

Dear Son,

An old man witnessed a butterfly struggling to emerge from his cocoon. It seemed that unless the young winged creature had help, he was doomed to die. So, with every good intention, the old man cupped his hands over the struggling butterfly and breathed, warm, moist air around what appeared to be a dying creature.

The moist air allowed the butterfly to slip away from the cocoon, but something was wrong. The cocoon struggle was meant to give the butterfly's wings time to dry; without the struggle the wings were useless. Now the old man could do nothing but watch the fragile creature die. In his attempt to rescue, he had denied the butterfly the life-giving benefits of the struggle.

Remember, you can't build faith without struggle. Don't be too quick to rescue. The struggle may be just what your kids need to develop their faith.

Love, Dad

# DEAR FATHER,

Help me understand that faith is more than just believing the right things about Jesus. Lord, help me to realize that faith has to be tested to grow, it has to have a struggle. And, Lord, help me learn how to listen to my kids when their faith struggle takes place, but keep me from rescuing them.

Lord, give me the opportunity to tell my kids my faith story. And, give my kids lots of opportunities to hear the faith stories of their teachers, and ministers, and friends.

Lord, help my kids not to stop after learning about the Scriptures. Help them to find wise ways to turn their knowledge into tested faith.

In Jesus' name, Amen.

1. What commitments do I need to make?

2. What action do I need to take?

3. What lesson can I pass on to my children?

*My son, keep your father's commands and do not forsake your mother's teaching.*

*Bind them upon your heart forever; fasten them around your neck.*

*When you walk, they will guide you; when you sleep, they will watch over you; when you awake, they will speak to you.*

*For these commands are a lamp, this teaching is a light,*

*and the corrections of discipline are the way to life,*

*keeping you from the immoral woman, from the smooth tongue of the wayward wife.*

*Do not lust in your heart after her beauty or let her captivate you with her eyes,*

*for the prostitute reduces you to a loaf of bread, and the adulteress preys upon your very life.*

Proverbs 6:20-26

# Talking About Sex

At times it may not seem like it, but as kids grow older they really do want to talk to their parents about their concerns. However, if you wait for your kids to ask you about the tough subjects, like sex, you may still be waiting after the grandchildren are having children.

I was taking a break between speeches at a conference on families when an excited young lady pulled me aside and asked for a moment of my time.

"I want to tell you about my dad," she said.

We sat down, and she began her story. "When I was in the seventh grade, Dad took me out to dinner. The food was good, but food wasn't the reason for this special night. He told me that he had something really important to talk about. Then he shared with me his secrets about boys. We talked about why boys are so thoughtless at times, about why they like to make loud, gross noises, about what they think about girls when they're with their friends, and what they think when they're with a girl.

"He explained how some boys will say anything to get sex from a girl, and he told me how to be a romantic virgin in a sexually active world.

"We talked for the rest of the evening," she said. "Don't you think I'm lucky to have a father like that?"

Yes, I do.

When my girls and I had our talk about dating, their first question was, "How far can I go and be safe?" or in other words, "Where should I draw the line?" This is *the* question.

In my answer, I wanted to set the stage, explain the theology, and list the reasons. My girls just wanted simple, uncomplicated advice.

In principle, here's what I said. "If you stay above the neck, you're safe. Below the neck can get you in trouble. I would have to be a cold-hearted block of ice to tell you never to kiss or be affectionate. If you like each other, you will want to be close, and you will want to kiss passionately. So here's my advice.

"Start slowly and be selective.

"Learn to draw the line and tell your date where the line is. Someday you'll thank God that's he made you with all this passion. But until that day, you need to draw a line and not cross it, no matter what.

"Keep hands outside the clothes. The minute you get your hands inside each other's clothes, you're headed for big trouble. Skin touching skin below the neck turns on passions you may not be able to control. Passion is like money; you always want more. What you do one night won't be enough for the next night."

Can you speak that way to your daughter, to your son? I hope you can. Our kids need all the help they can get, and they want the help to come from us. If you anticipate trouble talking this way to your kids, write your counsel in a letter and send it through the mail. I guarantee they will read the letter. Remember, no one has more influence in this area of your child's life than you do. So forget about the anatomy lesson and focus on sexual feelings, character, and the Spirit of God.

Dear Son,

Sex and romance are the two most difficult subjects to discuss. My dad tried to talk about sex one day. It was a couple hours before the wedding, and we had a quiet moment together. He asked if I had any questions and if I knew what to do. I responded like millions before me. "No questions," of course. "I know what to do." Both were bold-faced lies.

Our conversation didn't go much better, did it? I know you must have gotten tired of hearing so much about responsibility, but I had to try. Was it really that bad?

Start early! Tell your kids about modesty and pornography, about sexiness and sensuality, about character and control, about self-gratification and lust, about tenderness and sacrifice. Don't try to pack everything into "the" talk. Be ready for a bunch of little talks. It's much better that way. Tell them about marriage, and eventually, tell them about the pleasures of marital sex.

Love, Dad

# DEAR LORD,

Give my kids the strength to draw the line when it comes to sex. Help me to be sensitive to their feelings and their frustrations. Help me to remember what it felt like to be in love with passion.

Please give me the opportunities to talk about sex and sexuality often. Help me know what to say and when to say it. And most of all, Lord, help me to show my children what love is all about by the way I treat my wife.

Lord, help me to feel more comfortable talking about sex with my wife and my kids. Help me start today.

In Jesus' name, Amen.

1. What commitments do I need to make?

2. What action do I need to take?

3. What lesson can I pass on to my children?

_____

_____

_____

_____

_____

_____

_____

*See, I will send you the prophet Elijah before that great and dreadful day of the Lord comes. He will turn the hearts of the fathers to their children, and the hearts of the children to their fathers; or else I will come and strike the land with a curse.*

Malachi 4:5, 6

# Feeling the Warmth

In a 1992 survey of men's attitudes about fatherhood, the top three characteristics of a good father were:

1. *Being there for the children when they need advice.* Providing advice, guidance, and suggestions as the children ask for them is one of the hallmarks of fatherhood. A loving father's words of advice are remembered for a lifetime, even if they are not followed.

2. *Being emotionally available to provide support and tenderness when children need it.* Researchers have found that although both parents can affect a child's performance in school, those children with the most self-confidence seem to have dads who are the warmest and most enthusiastic when work is the toughest.

   Warm fathers have fun with the tasks, they enjoy the time they spend with each child, and they are openly affectionate.

   Warm fathers help kids feel accepted. And when kids feel accepted, regardless of how they do, they feel that they have more leeway to make mistakes, which helps them eventually master whatever they undertake.

3. *Spending time with the children,* but also working hard to provide for them. Ongoing studies on the influence of fathers have found that men who are nurturant—actively involved in everyday lives of their children—have children who develop a larger collection of social skills, are more flexible in stressful situations, and perform better on standardized tests. Think of it this way. Your time on the floor playing and reading with your child is helping prepare him for the future, even when you're having fun. And your investment while your children are young will pay great dividends later.

So, when you pull into the driveway after a long day at work, let the engine idle for a moment. Spend a few seconds warming up for the most important part of your day—family time.

Men also report that no matter how important their children are to them, most have trouble talking about their feelings of fathering. When asked what they talk to their peers about, fathering ranked last.

The order reported was:
1. Work
2. Sports
3. What the children are up to
4. Hobbies
5. Politics
6. Sex
7. Music
8. How I feel about being a father

I am convinced that fathers who spend time talking to other fathers about their feelings of being a father will be voted the best by those whose votes count most.

Dear Son,

Trust me, your child doesn't want to hear he's terrific when he knows he's messed up. He just wants to know that you still love him, no matter what.

When your child loses the election or doesn't make the starting lineup, don't ask "what happened" or "why" it happened. Your first words might be, "I know how important that was to you. Losing has to hurt worse than anything in the whole world." Hearing these words or words like them assures your child that he is understood and loved.

That's what being a warm father is all about.

Love, Dad

# DEAR FATHER,

Don't let me get so busy that I miss the childhood of my children. Help me to slow down, get involved, and stay aware. Give me the words to say that will convince my children I am concerned and that I am trying to understand.

Help me know how to help them when they're down.

Melt any part of my heart that is keeping me from becoming a warm father for each of my children.

In Jesus' name, Amen.

1. What commitments do I need to make?

2. What action do I need to take?

3. What lesson can I pass on to my children?

*So Joshua called together the twelve men he had appointed from the Israelites, one from each tribe, and said to them, "Go over before the ark of the Lord your God into the middle of the Jordan. Each of you is to take up a stone on his shoulder, according to the number of the tribes of the Israelites, to serve as a sign among you. In the future, when your children ask you, 'What do these stones mean?' tell them that the flow of the Jordan was cut off before the ark of the covenant of the Lord. When it crossed the Jordan, the waters of the Jordan were cut off. These stones are to be a memorial to the people of Israel forever."*

Joshua 4:4-7

# Celebrating Life

I know you have already heard about the Terrible Two's, that period from about eighteen months of age to around three years. Let me tell you about Robin—she's two. Robin's father, Ralph, is still in shock. This cute little two-year-old made an unforgettable impression on everyone in town.

Her trail of disasters began with the toilet. Alice, the cat, got dunked, drowned, and flushed. A few days later, Robin decided to give teddy bear a bath. She set him on top of the heating element in the dishwasher. The bear came out a limp, crispy critter. Robin then attacked the refrigerator. Just before the family took a weekend trip, she stuck some magnetic letters in the vents, causing the motor to burn out. The very next day, Robin's mother left her asleep in her car seat while she went in the post office to mail a letter. When she came out, she discovered Robin coasting the car into a nearby tree.

A week later, Robin's mom and dad parked their car halfway in the garage after a shopping trip because they were planning to unload groceries. Robin was strapped in the car seat, and her mother had the keys. While the parents were in the kitchen, they heard loud noises from the garage. When they got outside, they found the automatic garage door bouncing up and down on the hood of the car, with you-know-who inside pushing the button.

Within just a few weeks, Robin's damages totalled $2,296.37.

Robin's father celebrated her third birthday in style.

Gordon McDonald tells about a famous biographer who frequently mentioned the impact of one special fishing trip with his dad. On this trip they talked of life, faith, love, and dreams. It was the best day of the young boy's life. After the father died, a friend discovered his journal entry for that special day. It read simply, "Gone fishing with my son. Day wasted."

Fishing trips are never wasted days. They are celebrations of life, even if you don't feel it at the moment.

Columnist Ellen Goodman stated a few years ago, "We don't have to achieve to be accepted by our families. We just have to *be*. Our membership is not based on credentials, but on birth."

Family is where we get our sense of belonging. "We're not just clusters of people living in the same house," states Jim Dobson. "We're a family that's conscious of its uniqueness, of its personality, of its character, and of its heritage." Celebrate being a part of your family. "Families who treasure their traditions and rituals," says Dolores Curran, "seem automatically to have a sense of family. Traditions are the underpinning in such families, and these traditions are regarded as necessities, not frills."

We celebrate family by passing milestones, by taking trips, by just being together, and by developing our own unique collection of rituals and traditions. In one way, traditions force us to celebrate being family.

Dear Son,

Spend some time developing a number of family traditions. They will remind you how important family is; they help you discover who you are. Traditions give us something to celebrate. They force us to change our schedules and adjust our activities. Our traditions give us identity and an assurance that we belong in our family.

So, celebrate birthdays, Thanksgiving, Christmas, Valentine's Day, anniversaries, milestones, achievements, getting the sink unstopped, losing a pound, and homemade holidays. Traditions don't have to be stuffy, formal activities. They can be off-the-wall, never-heard-of-before experiences. The key is *how* we celebrate them.

Consider adding prayer to each of your traditions. This one simple act will bring a focus on God into your family activities and position you as the spiritual leader.

Ask your kids to plan a new family tradition. And go for it.

Love, Dad

# DEAR GOD,

Help me to find ways to celebrate family. Help me take the lead in developing traditions that will keep me focused on you. And help me learn how to celebrate our milestones, trips, and traditions in such a way that my kids will cherish the memories. Help me to include you in all our celebrations.

Help my kids learn about what's really important in life through our special times. And God, help me know when the fishing trip is special, because I don't want to waste a single day.

God, thank you for kids.

In Jesus' name, Amen.

1. What commitments do I need to make?

2. What action do I need to take?

3. What lesson can I pass on to my children?

Jesus continued: "There was a man who had two sons. The younger one said to his father, 'Father, give me my share of the estate.' So he divided his property between them.

"Not long after that, the younger son got together all he had, set off for a distant country and there squandered his wealth in wild living. After he had spent everything, there was a severe famine in that whole country, and he began to be in need. So he went and hired himself out to a citizen of that country, who sent him to his fields to feed pigs. He longed to fill his stomach with the pods that the pigs were eating, but no one gave him anything.

"When he came to his senses, he said, 'How many of my father's hired men have food to spare, and here I am starving to death! I will set out and go back to my father and say to him: Father, I have sinned against heaven and against you. I am no longer worthy to be called your son; make me like one of your hired men.' So he got up and went to his father.

"But while he was still a long way off, his father saw him and was filled with compassion for him; he ran to his son, threw his arms around him and kissed him.

"The son said to him, 'Father, I have sinned against heaven and against you. I am no longer worthy to be called your son.'

"But the father said to his servants, 'Quick! Bring the best robe and put it on him. Put a ring on his finger and sandals on his feet. Bring the fattened calf and kill it. Let's have a feast and celebrate. For this son of mine was dead and is alive again; he was lost and is found.' So they began to celebrate.

"Meanwhile, the older son was in the field. When he came near the house, he heard music and dancing. So he called one of the servants and asked him what was going on. 'Your brother has come,' he replied, 'and your father has killed the fattened calf because he has him back safe and sound.'

"The older brother became angry and refused to go in. So his father went out and pleaded with him. But he answered his father, 'Look! All these years I've been slaving for you and never disobeyed your orders. Yet you never gave me even a young goat so I could celebrate with my friends. But when this son of yours who has squandered your property with prostitutes comes home, you kill the fattened calf for him!'

"'My son,' the father said, 'you are always with me, and everything I have is yours. But we had to celebrate and be glad, because this brother of yours was dead and is alive again; he was lost and is found.'"

Luke 15:11-32

# Storytelling for Life

Everyone likes stories. When children are young, they love stories. They especially like the simple, familiar ones that parents are bored with. Then sometime before their fifth year, they want stories with heroes, action, and danger. Yes, and a happy ending.

When fathers become storybook readers and storytellers, they teach lessons that will last a lifetime. Reading or telling good stories captures attention, encourages imagination, defines character, underscores morality, tests conclusions, and builds closeness. Nothing is as effective in reaching your child's head and heart as is storytelling.

Reading or telling stories is not an alternative activity for strong fathers. It is a prerequisite. There is a blossoming storyteller locked inside every father, and his children deserve to have that trapped storyteller released and energized.

These suggestions will help fathers add warmth and coziness to their storytelling times:

1. ***Begin by reading good stories to your youngsters.*** Reading is not as effective as *telling* the story, but for most, it is an excellent way to start. The kids will love the familiar stories.

2. ***Become a collector of good children's storybooks.*** Ask librarians, bookstore managers, and parents for recommendations. This collection of storybooks will become a valued possession. Keep adding to it as the children grow older.

3. ***Take a chance.*** Try telling a story without the book. If you mess up, your child can help you out. Read the story several times so you get the sequence of events. Then just do it. Avoid memorizing the story. Telling the story in your own words allows you to adapt and take advantage of unexpected events and interruptions, like the dog jumping into your lap, or another child wanting to join in.

4. ***Tell your kids true-life stories from your past and other family stories.***

5. ***Make up stories about someone in your family.*** Remember, every family story should be about a hero who overcomes a difficulty and returns to the love and protection of home. By creating this series of stories, you can open conversations about heartfelt issues.

Stories help us understand life and how the pieces fit. If helping children understand life is one of a father's goals, then storytelling is the best way to get there.

Dear Son,

I remember that my dad's mother was a great storyteller. I loved to spend nights at their house. There was no television and no electricity. She would light a candle, and I would get a pillow to sit on. Then the adventure began. Most of the stories were the same time after time, but I loved the voices she used, and once in a while, she would make up a story about me or my dad. I'll never forget those evenings.

My dad told stories; most of them were told while we were up all night fishing for catfish. His stories were about when he was a youngster. Occasionally he would tell a scary story or two. I loved those. In fact, I have told *you* some of those stories. Remember?

Start a collection of good stories now. Keep a file of them, because believe it or not, you will forget the ones you don't tell very often. Even in the days of TV and computers, your kids will still love stories.

Don't forget the stories of the Bible. Pick out five or six of your favorite Bible stories and read them over and over until you've got the storyline down. Then tell it, in your own words. Don't read it; tell it. There is a time to read a story, and there is a time to tell it.

And please don't fall into the trap of buying some toy or tape recorder to be your substitute storyteller. They are fine in addition to you, but not as a substitute. They don't have your skin or your eyes or your hugs.

Love, Dad

# DEAR FATHER,

Release the storyteller inside me. Help me to tell stories that my kids will want to hear.

Help me to read and tell my children stories that will teach them about your love, about your grace, and about your Son.

Help me to tell them stories about faith and courage. And help them to remember the messages inside the stories.

In Jesus' name, Amen.

1. What commitments do I need to make?

2. What action do I need to take?

3. What lesson can I pass on to my children?

*When Jesus looked up and saw a great crowd coming toward him, he said to Philip, "Where shall we buy bread for these people to eat?" He asked this only to test him, for he already had in mind what he was going to do.*

*Philip answered him, "Eight months' wages would not buy enough bread for each one to have a bite!"*

*Another of his disciples, Andrew, Simon Peter's brother, spoke up, "Here is a boy with five small barley loaves and two small fish, but how far will they go among so many?"*

*Jesus said, "Have the people sit down." There was plenty of grass in that place, and the men sat down, about five thousand of them. Jesus then took the loaves, gave thanks, and distributed to those who were seated as much as they wanted. He did the same with the fish.*

*When they had all had enough to eat, he said to his disciples, "Gather the pieces that are left over. Let nothing be wasted." So they gathered them and filled twelve baskets with the pieces of the five barley loaves left over by those who had eaten.*

John 6:5-13

## Remembering Surprises

I f you want to do something that your children are sure to remember long after you are gone, try some random acts of kindness. You may think these are crazy ideas, but perhaps surprising our children with a little craziness is just the ticket for teaching them some of the most important values of life. In our self-focused society, it takes unusual methods to get the attention of our youngsters. What if your youngster was to witness the following incident?

Let's say you're the manager at a local sporting goods store and an aspiring young baseball star has been coming by the store for months. Each day he comes in, heads straight for the baseball area, and puts on the most expensive baseball mitt in the house. He pounds his fist into the pocket a couple times and then carefully puts it back on the shelf. He looks longingly at the glove, then turns and leaves. Each day you watch the boy's dream grow.

Then one day the boy brings in a shoe box full of nickels, quarters, and dimes. He pours it out in front of you; his stash adds up to exactly $19.98. The young dreamer believes this is the day, the day he'll take his glove home. But the mitt costs $79.98, plus tax.

Sure enough, the seven on the price tag is smudged just enough so that a hopeful seven-year-old could imagine it to be a one. You look at the youngster's smile and very carefully recount the money.

"Yep, exactly $19.98." You wrap up the mitt and give it to the boy.

Is that memory worth sixty dollars? What impact would it make on your child?

Imagine you and your child are having an early morning donut together at the local coffee shop. The waitress takes your order, and you and your child begin to talk about the day. Then, without warning you say to your child, "Want to have some fun? Watch this!" You call the young waitress over and tell her of your plan. You give her twenty dollars and tell her you are paying for the next ten coffees. Her job is to smile and tell people that their morning coffee has been paid for by a generous friend.

Then you sit back and watch the faces of the people. You see people look around for someone they know. You see some shake their heads in bewilderment. You see some smile and say thanks. You see one leave a dollar for someone else.

What does your child see?

You will have begun that day making a memorable impact on eleven people.

Dear Son,

Surprises are memory makers.

Get the kids to help you surprise their mother with a clean house, or a home-cooked meal, or a "we'll do the dishes after dinner" surprise.

Plan a camp out in the living room. Make tents out of blankets, bring snacks, cook hot dogs in the fireplace, tell stories, stay up late, and take pictures.

Take your children to breakfast just for the fun of it.

Get trash bags and clean up the neighborhood, not just your lot but the whole neighborhood.

Spend a morning cleaning graffiti off park benches. Plant wildflowers along the side of the road. Practice some guerrilla goodness.

Think of some surprisingly incredible thing to do, take your child with you, and let him experience the joy of random acts of kindness. Spread the message. Make some bumper stickers and business cards. Surprises, those focused inside your family and those focused outside your family, are catching.

Love, Dad

# DEAR LORD,

Sometimes, I forget that all the miracles were surprises. They were unexpected acts of kindness that changed people's lives. Help me to be more aware of when I can do the same.

Give me the wisdom to know what to do and when to do it. Help my children learn from each of the surprises.

Lord, I want my children to know that kindness is a surprise that is always appreciated and hopefully repeated.

Thank you for being a God of surprises.

In Jesus' name, Amen.

1. What commitments do I need to make?

2. What action do I need to take?

3. What lesson can I pass on to my children?

_____

_____

_____

_____

_____

_____

_____

_____

*Then the Jews who lived near them came and told us ten times over, "Wherever you turn, they will attack us."*

*Therefore I stationed some of the people behind the lowest points of the wall at the exposed places, posting them by families, with their swords, spears and bows. After I looked things over, I stood up and said to the nobles, the officials, and the rest of the people, "Don't be afraid of them. Remember the Lord, who is great and awesome, and fight for your brothers, your sons and your daughters, your wives and your homes."*

*When our enemies heard that we were aware of their plot and that God had frustrated it, we all returned to the wall, each to his own work.*

*From that day on, half of my men did the work, while the other half were equipped with spears, shields, bows and armor. The officers posted themselves behind all the people of Judah.*

Nehemiah 4:12-16

# Balancing Tasks

**D**oes this turmoil sound familiar? Tommy needs to eat dinner at 6:00 P.M. because of a school function at 7:00. His sister, Joy, must be picked up from her volleyball game at 7:15. Both children are upset because Mom has to be at an office function and won't be home until 8:15; thus, no dinner and no transportation. Dad was supposed to come to the rescue, but there's a problem at the Chicago office, and he has to fly there tonight. To complicate matters, tomorrow is Grandma's birthday, and no one remembered her card or present. As soon as Dad gets home, he discovers a phone message from an old friend who wants to drop by for the evening. And one of Mom's friends left a tearful message about her unraveling marriage. The bills have been collecting in the "bill drawer" for forty-five days. The lawn needs mowing, both cars need an oil change, and Dad has a nagging feeling he has forgotten something really important.

Have you been there? It's called life-on-tilt—everything is out of balance.

When our lives get off balance and our focus is on our frustration and on what isn't working, we get what my grandma used to call, "out of sorts."

Unfortunately, when many of us get "out of sorts," we respond with our same old methods and expect that, somehow, things will turn out differently. That's what I used to do. Now I'm convinced that's borderline insanity.

The following steps have helped me regain my balance, and they can help you too:

1. *Take time out.* Close your eyes and take four uninterrupted deep breaths.

2. *Spend a few moments in prayer.* Confess your readiness to overreact. Confess your frustration. Ask God to help you regain your balance and grow from this experience.

3. *Ask yourself,* "What do I need to change so I will get different results next time?"

4. *Ask yourself,* "What can I teach my child about how to get life back in balance when everything is 'out of sorts'?"

5. *Trust God* to show you the changes to make. Ask him to help you work on one change at a time. Then trust God, not your ability. Write your request on a card and keep the card with you at all times. Read it daily.

Remember, God works on his schedule, not yours.

Dear Son,

To your children, you are a great man whether you are a financial success or not. You shape their worldview, dispense discipline, teach object lessons, hand down spiritual and moral legacies. That's the big picture.

The little picture is filled with frustrations, pressures, doubts, and fears. We live day by day in the little picture, hoping one day to see the big picture.

By the time I realized what I needed to do to correct my mistakes as a father, you kids were grown. You and I just have to learn to live with the consequences. I kept trying to rescue you from the mistakes I had made, and I had this strange desire to push you through childhood, as though there was something wrong with being a kid.

Maybe we would all do better if we'd just relax and enjoy where we are at the moment. Why is that so difficult to do when you're an adult?

I still need God to help me get my focus off myself and onto him. Only when my focus is off me do I find balance.

That's the real blessing of being in God's family. He's a perfect father for both of us.

Love, Dad

# DEAR GOD,

There are times when my life is beyond tilt. I seem to get off balance all the time. Things just seem to get out of control. Maybe I need more time alone with you.

God, when work and family and church and sports and you-know-what get all mixed up, help me learn to back off and get in touch with you. I need the balance you bring to my life.

And help me teach my children how to stay in balance, too. Help all of us to get our focus off ourselves and on you.
In Jesus' name, Amen.

1. What commitments do I need to make?

2. What action do I need to take?

3. What lesson can I pass on to my children?

For, "Whoever would love life and see good days must keep his tongue from evil and his lips from deceitful speech.

He must turn from evil and do good; he must seek peace and pursue it.

For the eyes of the Lord are on the righteous and his ears are attentive to their prayer,

but the face of the Lord is against those who do evil."


1 Peter 3:10-12

# Achieving Peace

There are days when the most illusive treasure in life is peace. I'm not talking about the lack-of-conflict peace; I'm talking about personal peace of mind in spite of the conflict. I believe fathers can lead the way in relcaiming the path to peace. Somehow there will always be tension between peace and risk, comfort and adventure, struggle and faith. There will always be threats to our peace.

While in graduate school, I participated in a project that researched what social scientists have discovered about the development of peace of mind. After combing through dozens of studies, we summarized our findings in these eight factors for achieving peace of mind.

1. *Rid yourself of suspicion and resentment.* Nursing a grudge is a major factor in unhappiness.

2. *Don't live in the past.* Preoccupation with old mistakes leads to personal discouragement and paralyzing depression.

3. *Cooperate with life.* Don't waste time fighting conditions you cannot change.

4. *Force yourself to stay involved* with the real world. Resist the temptation to withdraw into your own private world.

5. *Refuse to indulge in self-pity.* Nobody gets through life without some misfortune along the way.

6. *Cultivate old-fashioned virtues.* Love, honor, compassion, loyalty, and integrity are always in style.

7. *Don't expect too much of yourself.* Develop realistic goals.

8. *Find something bigger than yourself to believe in.* Keep your life focus outside yourself.

These eight factors are helpful and straightforward, but the real answer to peace is not found in all the collective wisdom of our social scientists. It is beyond us; it is beyond our understanding. Try as we may to figure out some social way of manufacturing peace, God is the only source. He makes peace out of the strangest things—like momentary frustrations, unexpected failures, loss of direction, personal pain, and family conflict.

Perhaps the greatest unclaimed gift God has given to his people is peace of mind. He provides it in unexpected ways. He surprises at unforeseen times. He takes the everyday moments of our lives and turns them into memories. He takes the ordinary and transforms it into the extraordinary. And he takes our insecurities and fears and gives us peace.

We give him our hopes and dreams, our children, our marriage, and he gives us purpose and grace and the desires of our heart that we haven't even thought of yet.

Make sure your family knows the God of peace—our Father-God.

Dear Son,

I know a dad who, when the pressure's on, can't relax. He turns his family into a project to be managed. He takes charge, dispenses orders, and solves problems, whether anyone wants him to or not. He has yet to discover the peace that passes understanding, although he can quote the verse.

I pray that you will learn to use the pressure times to connect with your kids and manage yourself. After all, we may be at our best when we are playing catch or listening to dreams. When your peace is threatened, it's time to focus on God. Get away to a park, a hillside, or quiet corner and pray.

Keep focusing outside yourself. Do something special with your kids. Tomorrow they'll be big. Go fishing, play catch, go hiking, or take a wilderness trek together. Try camping or take an overnight trip. Whatever you do, don't solve any problems. Don't try to get new information. Just have lots of meandering conversation. Oh, and take lots of pictures. Getting lost in these moments will help you refocus priorities and reclaim God's gift of peace. Does that sound mysterious? It is!

Some of my best memories of your childhood started out as threats to my peace of mind and ended up as moments spent on the floor playing a game, reading a book, or just giggling together.

How about you?

Love, Dad

# DEAR FATHER,

I want to turn my family over to you. I want us to serve you, to worship you, and to help others find you. And I want your gift of peace, the peace that is beyond explanation and understanding.

Lord, I need peace right now in so many areas of my life. Help me to view every experience of my life as an opportunity to claim your gift of peace.

Lord, forgive my self-directedness. Forgive my self-reliance. Forgive my self-focus. Give me a vision beyond myself and help me to pass that vision on to my family.

Help my kids learn to claim your peace early in their lives.

And, Lord, help us live one day at a time.

In Jesus' name, amen.

---

1. What commitments do I need to make?

2. What action do I need to take?

3. What lesson can I pass on to my children?

_____

_____

_____

_____

_____

_____